"Dr. Bradley consistently brings poignant insights into the Christian, black, and hip-hop communities. Here he gives worldview-shifting challenges and profound, timeless solutions. I'm grateful to know him and have this book in my hands."

LeCrae Moore, hip-hop artist, Rehab Records

"*Keep Your Head Up* challenges the churches not to let traditions and culture keep them from missing the past two generations of young people who have been unchurched. Bradley encourages the church to be intentional in building open, listening relationships with those who have been influenced by hip-hop and gangsta rap. The church must become more user-friendly to these dear ones in our communities."

Donovan E. Case, President, African Americans For Missions (AAFM)

"Dr. Bradley's call for psychological *and* spiritual wholeness is a daring, needed charge to our ethnic communities. It is my hope that the thorough brand of freedom he envisions will accompany the resurgence of the gospel in our cities and families."

Jason Wright, 7-year NFL veteran; MBA Candidate, University of Chicago, Booth School of Business

"*Keep Your Head Up* is candid, convicting, and balanced. Bradley assembles a great team of Christian thinkers who create a dialog between Augustine, Bell, Hooks, Ice Cube, and William Julius Wilson on one hand and Bill Cosby, Alvin Poussaint, and Eric Michael Dyson on the other. The writers provide great cultural, statistical, and historical analysis of the *Come On, People* and *Is Bill Cosby Right?* approaches to complex social issues within Black America and of how far we have to go to overcome. Along the way, they redefine black church, black theology, and what it means to be African-American, producing a fresh new call for the church to hear the truth. This is a significant discussion needed in every church in America so that the 'One New Man' can solve the institutionalized and self-inflicted problems facing the African-American community. This work demonstrates that the applied gospel in the hands of the church of Jesus Christ is sufficient to meet the needs of a community that often still faces the reality of living in a present hell."

Eric C. Redmond, author, *Where Are All the Brothers?: Straight Answers to Men's Questions about the Church*

"There has been an epidemic among African-Americans for many generations. I am excited that this book highlights the reality of the epidemic from a Christ-centered paradigm, focusing on him and not the false American dream of 'pulling yourself up by your bootstraps.' I pray this book alarms the redeemed to the reality of this call. This is a generational issue that beckons the talents, resources, visions, and gifts from the body of Christ at large."

Adam Thomason, Lead Teaching Pastor, Damascus Road, Flint, Michigan; author, *Red Revolution: Seeing the World Through the Lens of Christ*

KEEP YOUR HEAD UP

ALSO BY ANTHONY B. BRADLEY:

Liberating Black Theology: The Bible and the Black Experience in America

Black and Tired: Essays on Race, Politics, Culture, and International Development

KEEP YOUR HEAD UP

AMERICA'S NEW BLACK CHRISTIAN LEADERS, SOCIAL CONSCIOUSNESS, AND THE COSBY CONVERSATION

ANTHONY B. BRADLEY, EDITOR

CROSSWAY

WHEATON, ILLINOIS

ISBN-13: 978-1-4335-0673-4
ISBN-10: 1-4335-0673-4
PDF ISBN: 978-1-4335-0674-1
Mobipocket ISBN: 978-1-4335-0675-8
ePub ISBN: 978-1-4335-2280-2

Library of Congress Cataloging-in-Publication Data
Keep your head up : America's new Black Christian leaders, social consciousness, and the Cosby conversation / Anthony B. Bradley, editor.
       p. cm.
   Includes bibliographical references.
   ISBN 978-1-4335-0673-4 (tp)
   1. African Americans—Religion. 2. African Americans—Social conditions. 3. Church and social problems—United States.
I. Bradley, Anthony B., 1971–   .
BR563.N4K443   2012
277.3'08308996073—dc22   2010053229

Crossway is a publishing ministry of Good News Publishers.
VP   21   20   19   18   17   16   15   14   13   12
14   13   12   11   10   9   8   7   6   5   4   3   2   1

To

Rev. Michael Jones

Pastor of Friendly Temple Missionary Baptist Church,
St. Louis, Missouri, and the entire Friendly Temple church
family for preaching and living the gospel in St. Louis.
Under Pastor Jones's dynamic leadership, Friendly Temple
continues to display the power and beauty of the gospel that
changes lives and transforms communities.

CONTENTS

Acknowledgments   11

List of Contributors   13

Preface   17

1   More Than Victims: The Benefits of a Theological Vision   21
    Vincent Bacote

2   The Black Family: The Hope of "True Religion"   41
    Bruce Fields

3   Sexuality in the Black Community   61
    Howard Brown

4   Gangsta Rap Made Me Do It: What's Really Goin' On?   81
    Ralph C. Watkins

5   Black Men and Masculinity   99
    Eric M. Mason

6   The Church and Community   119
    Lance Lewis

7   Redeemed and Healed for Mission   137
    Anthony B. Bradley

8   The Black Church and Orthodoxy   157
    Anthony Carter

9   The Prosperity Gospel   177
    Ken Jones

10 Rev. Michael Eric Dyson: An Analysis   197
    Craig Mitchell

Conclusion   215

General Index   219

Scripture Index   221

ACKNOWLEDGMENTS

The contributors and I have worked on this book for a long time, and we are grateful to have the project in print. This project would not be possible were it not for the great team at Crossway Books— Al Fisher, Justin Taylor, Jill Carter, and the editors at Crossway.

I am very thankful for Marvin Olasky, former Provost at the King's College, for providing office space and resources to bring this project to a close during my year as a visiting Professor of Theology. My King's College student editorial team of Matthew Rosenbaum and Daniel Hay both did a superb job with the initial copy editing. Finally, Lori Niehoer showed editorial brilliance by working so hard to make all the contributors read well.

LIST OF CONTRIBUTORS

Vincent Bacote is Associate Professor of Theology and Director of the Center for Applied Christian Ethics at Wheaton College in Wheaton, Illinois. He earned a PhD from Drew University, an MPhil from Drew University, an MDiv from Trinity Evangelical Divinity School, and a BS in biology from The Citadel. He is the author of *The Spirit in Public Theology: Appropriating the Legacy of Abraham Kuyper.*

Anthony B. Bradley is Associate Professor of Theology and Ethics at the King's College, New York City, and a Research Fellow at the Acton Institute for the Study of Religion and Liberty. He holds a PhD from Westminster Theological Seminary, an MDiv from Covenant Theological Seminary, and a BS in biological sciences from Clemson University. Bradley is the author of *Liberating Black Theology: The Bible and the Black Experience in America* and *Black and Tired: Essays on Race, Politics, Culture, and International Development.*

Howard Brown is pastor of Christ Central Church in Charlotte, North Carolina. Rev. Brown holds an MDiv from Covenant Theological Seminary and a BA in English from Clemson University.

Anthony Carter is lead pastor of East Point Church in East Point, Georgia. Rev. Carter received an MA in biblical studies at Reformed Theological Seminary and a BA from Atlanta Christian College. He is the author of several books including *On Being Black and Reformed: A New Look at the African-American Christian Experience* and is the general editor of *Experiencing the Truth: Bringing the Reformation to the African-American Church* and *Glory Road: The Journeys of 10 African-Americans into Reformed Christianity.*

Bruce Fields is Associate Professor of Biblical and Systematic Theology at Trinity Evangelical Divinity School in Deerfield, Illinois. He earned a PhD in New Testament at Marquette University, an MDiv from Trinity Evangelical Divinity School, a ThM in systematic theology from Trinity Evangelical Divinity School, and a BA in biology from the University of Pennsylvania. He is the author of *Black Theology: 3 Crucial Questions for the Evangelical Church.*

Ken Jones is the pastor of Glendale Baptist Church in Miami, Florida, and co-host of the nationally syndicated radio program *White Horse Inn.* Rev. Jones has contributed essays in *Experiencing the Truth* and *Glory Road,* both published by Crossway. He has also contributed to *Tabletalk* magazine and is a frequent conference speaker.

Lance Lewis is pastor of Christ Liberation Fellowship in Philadelphia. Rev. Lewis holds an MDiv from Chesapeake Theological Seminary and a BA in English from Temple University.

Eric M. Mason is cofounder and lead pastor of Epiphany Fellowship in Philadelphia. Mason received a DMin from Gordon-Conwell Theological Seminary and a ThM from Dallas Theological Seminary.

Craig Mitchell is Associate Professor of Ethics, Chair of the Ethics Department, and Associate Director of the Richard Land Center for Cultural Engagement, Southwestern Baptist Theological Seminary, Fort Worth, Tx. He has a PhD in Christian ethics from Southwestern Baptist Theological Seminary, an MDiv from Southwestern Baptist Theological Seminary, an MA in management information systems from West Coast University, an MS in engineering management from West Coast University and in electrical engineering from Naval Postgraduate School, and a BS in electronic engineering technology from Savannah State College. He is the author of *Charts for Philosophies and Philosophers* and *Charts of Christian Ethics.*

Ralph C. Watkins is Associate Professor of Evangelism and Church Growth, Columbia Theological Seminary, Decatur, GA.

He earned a PhD from the University of Pittsburgh, a DMin from Pittsburgh Theological Seminary, an MA from the University of Dubuque Theological Seminary, and a BA from California State University at Sacramento. He is author of *The Gospel Remix: Reaching the Hip Hop Generation*, *I Ain't Afraid to Speak My Mind*, *From Jay-Z to Jesus: Reaching and Teaching Young Adults in the Black Church* (coauthored with Benjamin Stephens), and *Hip Hop Redemption: Finding God in the Music and the Message*.

PREFACE

The black community is in trouble. Some might even call it a crisis. This book is a continuation of the conversation started by Bill Cosby and Alvin Poussaint, MD, two sages in the black community, in the 2007 book *Come On People: On the Path from Victims to Victors*. Cosby and Poussaint did not mince words in speaking about the state of black men and the social pathologies wreaking havoc in low-income black neighborhoods, including children not being parented well, children suffering in substandard public education, media that glory in the dehumanization of women and men, unhealthy eating habits, black-on-black violence, and lack of economic empowerment. *Come on People* was an honest challenge for blacks from all walks of life to pay attention to a group of Americans that have been ignored by many, including the black middle class. Taking this even further, we believe that we will not make progress until we hear from black religious leaders who hold the work and person of Christ in high esteem.

Historically the black church has been a place of spiritual formation and cultural renewal in the black communities. Because the church remains relevant today, that tradition must continue because people need help and hope. The election of Barack Obama to the presidency of the United States was a wonderful example of social progress but can only offer limited hope to address the deeply differentiated social and spiritual issues that have many black communities in America in a new kind of oppression. We need to hear from the Lord. We have assembled some of the most dynamic and progressive black pastors and theologians in America to move this conversation forward because we believe the church must lead in initiating the type of renewal needed to rightly answer the deep questions about solutions to the crisis.

In chapter 1 Vincent Bacote sets the stage for this new movement by addressing the issue of African-American identity and the victim mentality that Cosby and Poussaint discuss in their book. Bacote sets the dynamic realities of personhood and dignity in a theological framework that seeks to establish the best framework for understanding the human person in light of God's intention for human life. In chapter 2 Bruce Fields provides a powerful vision for strengthening the black family to cast a vision and offer hope for redeeming the most important social institution in black communities. Without strong black families there is not much hope for sustainable change. Howard Brown, in chapter 3, writes forthrightly about sex and sexuality in the black community. Some of the issues Cosby and Poussaint addressed reveal the consequences of divorcing sexuality from the covenant of marriage.

Is there anything redeemable about hip-hop? Can we learn anything from the genre that might help us know how to help people? These questions and more will be addressed in chapter 4 by Ralph Watkins. The celebration of misogyny, violence, and materialism in popular hip-hop provides an easy target for criticism. Cosby and Poussaint point out many of the negative aspects of the music. What may not be so clear, however, is that hip-hop provides signals of pain and suffering that we certainly do not want to miss if we want to accurately apply the gospel to the sin and brokenness experienced in daily life for many African-Americans. Additionally, popular hip-hop presents an image of what it means to be a black male in America that the gospel needs to address. Eric Mason, in chapter 5, "keeps it real" by challenging the distorted vision of black masculinity in our culture and provides a way forward in light of the gospel. The first five chapters are crucial for providing a gospel-driven framework to reconstruct a black identity with meaning and purpose that is in harmony with the realization of the good purposes for human life.

Does the church have any role to play in healing the black community? Since the time of American slavery black churches in

America served as the cement that kept communities and families together within the context of oppression. The church has a central mission to provide the spiritual formation necessary to ignite virtuous social mores in communities and has been doing so for centuries. Lance Lewis, in chapter 6, discusses the redemptive power that local churches can have in helping communities wrestle with complicated issues. In chapter 7, using Isaiah 61:1–4, I introduce readers to a vision of gospel transformation that takes broken people on a journey to liberation with a life redirected to the kingdom in order to become victors and agents of mercy, justice, and faithfulness to the priorities of the mission of God. In chapter 8 Anthony Carter, with great clarity and insight, addresses the need for biblical orthodoxy in black churches if the church intends to be what it always has been for black people and the world: the central destination for renewal.

One of the greatest impediments to the healthy mission of the black church has been the rise of the prosperity gospel. The prosperity gospel has devastated the lives of many people who need help from God by distorting the core message of the gospel. In chapter 9 Ken Jones discusses the prosperity gospel in historical context and offers important biblical and theological corrections to a movement that has exploded in black communities all over America. We conclude the book by introducing readers to Michael Eric Dyson, an ordained Baptist minister and professor of sociology at Georgetown University. Dyson has been one of the most outspoken academic critics of Bill Cosby's vision to move African-Americans away from a victim mentality to one of personal empowerment. The author of sixteen books to date, with more surely to come, Dyson has emerged as a leading voice on helping the black community, often wedding biblical themes with themes in popular hip-hop. In chapter 10 Craig Mitchell provides an introduction to Dyson for readers and provides a theological evaluation of Dyson to put him in biblical perspective.

It is my hope that this book will be read critically and will create new questions for a national dialogue about the black church and her connection to the black community as we move forward. I and the other contributors to this book are all independent thinkers from multiple traditions. While we do not agree on specific prescriptions for change in all areas, we do share a central conviction that there needs to be a resurgence of black religious leadership to properly address the issues that plague the community and every individual person in it. We hope this will be the first step in rallying black religious leaders to lock arms and provide the moral voice that our communities and the world desperately need. There is much work to do, and there is no time to waste. It's time to "get real."

Anthony B. Bradley
The King's College

1

MORE THAN VICTIMS: THE BENEFITS OF A THEOLOGICAL VISION

Vincent Bacote

Bill Cosby and Alvin Poussaint's *Come On People: On the Path from Victims to Victors* sounds an alarm about a crisis in the African-American[1] community. The subtitle suggests that this emergency situation can be construed as an identity crisis, at least in part. From the vantage point of Cosby and Poussaint, a victim identity and/or mentality only facilitates and entrenches the crisis at hand. How should we think about African-American identity, particularly when we look at it through a theological lens? This chapter will first look with Cosby and Poussaint at the circumstances that have given rise to a victim mentality and some of the responses to Cosby and Poussaint and then will consider a vision of African-American identity rooted in some of the categories we find in the biblical narrative.

ELEMENTS OF THE CRISIS

The subtitle of *Come On People* reveals the desire to promote a positive African-American identity. In order to properly address the issue of identity, we must accompany the authors as they address the various challenges that have led some (perhaps many) to see themselves as victims. Each chapter of the Cosby/Poussaint book addresses a particular set of problems. My first task is to identify

---

[1]In this chapter I will use both *African-American* and *black* as labels.

the elements from each chapter that can comprise a victim identity. The path to a helpful theological response requires us to face the various aspects of this dilemma with a clear, unadulterated vision.

Cosby and Poussaint begin with the crisis of the African-American male. Linked to lamentable community decline and a loss of parental skills, the plight of African-American men has emerged unexpectedly. In spite of the legal protections from segregation and discrimination won in the civil rights era, a new legacy of success in mainstream America has not emerged, particularly for those inhabiting a lower economic station. A startling change has occurred:

> In 1950, five out of every six black children were born into a two-parent home. Today, that number is less than two out of six. In poor communities, that number is lower still. There are whole blocks with scarcely a married couple, whole blocks without responsible males to watch out for wayward boys, whole neighborhoods in which little girls and boys come of age without seeing up close a committed partnership and perhaps never having attended a wedding.[2]

For African-American males, this drastic shift in poor communities has set the stage for a number of specific problems. Chief among these is the absence of fathers. While there are many virtuous and strong black women in these communities, this fails to adequately compensate for the vacuum of positive male influence within families. The effects of this absence reverberate broadly from deficient visions of success to education to dating. The following list presents some of the worst results:

- Homicide is the number one cause of death for African-American males aged fifteen to twenty-nine.
- Black men commit more than half of the homicides each year.
- Regarding what is known as "black on black" murder, in 94 percent of black homicides both victim and assailant are black.

---

[2]Bill Cosby and Alvin Poussaint, MD, *Come On People: On the Path from Victims to Victors* (Nashville: Thomas Nelson, 2007), 2.

- There is a lower average life expectancy (sixty-nine years) for African-American males.
- The suicide rate among blacks has increased more than 100 percent in recent decades.
- High school dropout rates by black males are more than 50 percent in some cities.
- Young black men have double the rate of unemployment compared to Caucasian, Asian, and Hispanic males.
- Forty-four percent of the prison population is black (African-Americans are 12 percent of the general population).
- Generally one in four black males is part of the criminal justice system.
- Six of ten high school dropouts have spent time in prison by their thirties.
- Approximately one-third of the homeless are black men.

Most of the men who fit the criminal statistics went afoul of the law because of drug activity, thievery, or gun violence, and the number has grown dramatically in recent decades. In spite of Daniel Patrick Moynihan's prediction about the effects of the welfare system, it is unlikely that anyone would have expected the effects to be so devastating.

Cosby and Poussaint identify other problems beyond criminality, such as the emotional problems that lie beneath a veneer of "coolness," the contrasting tendency to resort to violence upon the slightest hint of "getting dissed," careless sexual promiscuity that leads to unplanned pregnancies (and men with no interest in responsible fatherhood), and mutual disrespect between men and women in romantic relationships (sometimes with the consequence of abused male children in fatherless homes).

The second chapter has a specific focus on community and explicitly draws attention to the detrimental effects of the myth of white supremacy on black identity. One prominent manifestation of this is the tendency to equate education and success with "being white." While acknowledging the role of systemic racism in United States history, Cosby and Poussaint are more concerned with the effects of white supremacy on the self-esteem of many African-Americans. The internalization of negative stereotypes and the tendency to live down to the expectations of low education and criminality along with other forms of failure facilitate and catalyze a form of mental inertia within youth; the authors wonder if this has meant accepting the lie that an entire culture primarily produces bottom-dwellers. The central concern in the entire chapter is the failure of communities to function as a village that supports its members and encourages even the most downtrodden to move toward success. It is particularly interesting that the church does not escape Cosby and Poussaint's critical gaze. While they do not universally criticize the church, they make the point that many churches have failed to encourage their congregants to tend to their communities as an expression of the mandate for humans to care for God's world. Put differently, the church is failing to combat the rampant victim mentality that immobilizes the range of responsibility necessary to have flourishing neighborhoods in spite of the challenges of the past.

Children are the focus of the third chapter, which begins with an emphasis on the responsibility of child care, though the specific focus is on parenting. In their efforts to prompt readers to elevate themselves beyond a victim mentality, Cosby and Poussaint address a combination of ignorance, neglect, and pathology that has conspired to keep African-Americans from flourishing. They proceed from the womb through the teen years and begin by drawing attention to a range of concerns such as proper prenatal and postpartum care, the role of nurture and positive attention, and the virtue of patience in parenting. The absence of such vital modes of care leads to children that struggle to thrive. These are the children who enter the educational system already at a disadvantage. Cosby and Poussaint also criticize physical punishment as an approach to discipline, particularly because such expressions can escalate to abusive violence and send the message that violence is the way to resolve problems. While not asserting that physical punishment inevitably leads to a broken spirit, the clear argument is that this approach to discipline can play a role in creating certain kinds of victims rather than producing productive citizens: "We're not saying that parents who occasionally spank children will damage them. The adults who feel spankings helped them were more likely to be the ones who were occasionally spanked. Unfortunately, those who were spanked excessively or abused as children are less likely to show up in our audiences as responsible adults."[3] Physical violence is not the only concern; verbal, sexual, spousal, and sibling abuse are also parts of a larger problem. The hope is that less violence of any kind in the home will reduce criminal violence elsewhere. A final notable concern in this chapter is self-concept. What concept of identity do parents convey? Is there shame related to skin color, beauty standards, education, and language? How many parents are unwitting allies in the construction of an identity of black victimhood and inferiority?

The fourth chapter, focused on education, might be understood in part as a lament that learning has somehow become linked to a bad public relations campaign. The authors state that apart from a well-trod path of educational uplift, "most of us would still be struggling at the fringes of society. Given this glorious history, it troubles us that so many black youths are as thrilled about getting an education as they are about getting head lice."[4] Why the lack of interest in getting a good education? Bad schools in poor areas, homes and communities that rouse little interest or inspiration for learning, low literacy and high dropout rates are not the components of good advertising for education; yet this is the context in which many poor blacks live every day. While Cosby and Poussaint trace a path toward uplift, the lived experience of many in such settings is comprised of an existence where it is "normal" to have little chance to be educated and have successful lives.

Media is the topic of the fifth chapter. After the success of positive programs such as *The Cosby Show* and *Roc*, the return of negative stereotypes through certain Hollywood films and music videos

---

[3]Ibid., 70.
[4]Ibid., 101.

along with the tendency to connect beauty with lower concentrations of melanin disheartens. The pervasiveness of violence, careless and promiscuous sexual behavior, and a disturbing proliferation of the N-word from the mouths of some black entertainers washes over the minds of African-American children in wave after wave of media. Models of decadence, self-destruction, and self-hatred are marketed, packaged, and sold to youths who often imitate the "reality" presented by their favorite celebrities. The role of advertising is also challenging. One example: some very popular celebrities promote liquor in magazines and television shows marketed to black communities. The authors point to research that shows a greater likelihood that children exposed to such ads will drink alcohol heavily. While media is not detrimental by definition, many films, video games, television programs, and websites wield great influence, often negatively.

The domain of health care is covered in the sixth chapter. Discrepancies in health care are one legacy of racism that continues to this day, in spite of a notable decrease in discriminatory practices in medicine. While the era of uninformed participation in research protocols is now past, a lingering distrust of the medical profession remains. I can attest to this personally. My mother had a basic distrust of the medical profession because of the many people she knew who received substandard health care, especially the elderly. This suspicion may have been a factor in the late discovery of the disease that killed her. The chapter indicates that deaths from cancer are also linked to the tendency to wait until it is too late for a proper diagnosis. Cosby and Poussaint note that this is quite typical for the black poor who don't have insurance or access to adequate care. For the black population overall, life expectancy is lower for males and females compared to their white counterparts, and the top seven causes of death are heart disease, cancer, stroke, diabetes, accidents, homicide, and HIV/AIDS. Passivity about health is as much of a problem as suspicion of the medical profession; ignorance combined with inadequate vigilance about diet and exercise contributes to a range of problems from tooth decay to diabetes to cancer. Mental health is perhaps a greater area of crisis because of a lack of awareness and understanding of depression and the stigma associated with mental illness in black communities. Unsound bodies and minds are certain roadblocks to abundant life.

The specter of violence appears in several chapters but gets direct focus in chapter 7. In the past many in the South projected their own violent behaviors onto black men, and the stereotype of the dangerous, sexually predatory, stupid, and violent black male prevails in the minds of many today. Though black crime against whites is relatively rare, there is indeed much crime and violence within black communities that suggests that black men are prone to violence. A glance at the statistics listed above from the first chapter reveals an epidemic. Although there has been a decrease in violence in recent years, this hardly means that the core problems have seriously abated. Deficient parenting, gangs as stand-ins for family units, drug culture, access to and use of guns, and disrespect for authority (particularly the police) mix together in communities in a cocktail that often produces violence.

The final chapter charts a course from poverty to prosperity. The topics from the previous chapters often contribute to poverty. "There are many causes of poverty among African-Americans, some direct and some indirect. Here is a partial list: institutional racism, limited job opportunities, low minimum wage, mental illness, physical disabilities, drug and alcohol abuse, lack of a high school diploma, incarceration, and a criminal record."[5] The authors admit that these are challenging conditions for anyone; but their message is that such conditions need not guarantee a life below the poverty line. Yet this struggle remains today.

Here is what many African-Americans live with every day: black males as an endangered species, unstable communities, children subject to poor parenting, deficient education, seductive and misleading media, poor health, excessive violence, and poverty. The relentless drumbeat of these elements would make anyone perceive

---

[5]Ibid., 223.

himself or herself as a victim; yet Cosby and Poussaint believe that these factors do not need to have the last word. While it is beyond dispute that the legacy of racism and white supremacy has victimized the black community, the central question of identity focuses on whether a legacy of oppression has the definitive voice. Adam Serwer's review of Claude Steele's *Whistling Vivaldi* helps us see some of the difficulty. Here are notable observations quoted at length:

> Racial identity . . . affects people's thinking and action in countless ways but often without any awareness or malice. People pick up on cues—a topic of conversation, the language used in an employment brochure, the number of people of their own race or gender in a classroom or office—and react on the basis of internalized concerns about being stereotyped. While people in every group register these signals, members of racial minorities often experience a threat—what Steele calls "stereotype" or "identity" threat—that impairs their performance. . . .
>
> In *Whistling Vivaldi*, Steele primarily focuses on underperforming college students, particularly blacks and women, who by reaching college might be thought to have conquered negative stereotypes. But the research that Steele and others have done indicates that when facing identity threat—that is, when they are reminded of the shortcomings associated with their group—these students tend to underperform in comparison to their male or white counterparts with similar scores. . . .
>
> Steele's experiments show that identity threat can affect a member of any group given the right context, but minorities and women face more of a problem because the stereotypes that work against them are so deeply rooted in our culture. The stress caused by identity threat then becomes an ever-present burden. Steele points to high rates of diseases such as hypertension among African-Americans as an example of the physiological effects of coping with identity threat on a constant basis. . . .
>
> *Whistling Vivaldi* conveys an understanding of why race remains such a powerful factor even in a society where racial discrimination is seen as abhorrent and prohibited by law. And

while Steele's research gives some measure of hope, I'm not betting that people would change even if they learned about his findings. Dealing with stereotype threat requires a willingness to admit the power that group identities have over our minds and actions, and most of us don't believe that we're susceptible to bias, whether we're the guy whistling classical music or the person sighing with relief and deciding not to cross the street.[6]

The legacy of white supremacy has tenacious and lingering effects that explicitly and implicitly penetrate the consciousness of many African-Americans. This at least suggests that an identity as a victim of some sort can be present even in those who are not in circumstances as dire as those presented in *Come On People*. The goal of this chapter is to present a theological path toward a more whole, positive, and responsible identity. Before bringing a theological voice to this conversation, however, we briefly turn to some of the responses to Cosby.

TALKING BACK TO BILL

It is important to remember that the response to Bill Cosby (there has been far less criticism of Alvin Poussaint) is not only to *Come on People* but also to his famous 2004 speech given at the fiftieth anniversary commemoration of the *Brown v. Topeka Board of Education* decision (called "the Pound Cake speech" by some). In that speech Cosby criticized irresponsibility in the black community, particularly in poorer areas. The speech attracted much affirmation and criticism: was this a matter of someone finally telling the truth, or was this yet another example of class warfare where upper- and middle-class blacks look down on and leave behind the underclass they hold in disdain? One of the most notable respondents was Michael Eric Dyson, who wrote the book *Is Bill Cosby Right? Or Has the Black Middle Class Lost Its Mind?* (2005). In various media Dyson took Cosby to task for "blaming the victim" and for

---

[6]Adam Serwer, "Our Racial Interior," review of *Whistling Vivaldi: And Other Clues to How Stereotypes Affect Us (Issues of Our Time)* by Claude M. Steele, *The American Prospect*, April 9, 2010; http://www.prospect.org/cs/articles?article=our_racial_interior.

betraying those still subject to an unfair society. *Come On People* was published in 2007, and some regard it as a response to the initial criticisms. That book was also subject to affirmation and critique. In addition to Dyson, other critics primarily focused on Cosby. They felt he used flawed data and preached about responsibility without taking into account the structural problems that have inhibited the success of many African-Americans. For example, Earl Ofari Hutchinson stated the following on the website The Huffington Post:

> [Cosby] did not qualify or provide a complete factual context for his blanket indictment of poor blacks. He made the negative behavior of some blacks a racial rather than an endemic social problem. In doing so, he did more than break the alleged taboo against publicly airing racial dirty laundry; he fanned dangerous and destructive stereotypes.
>
> This is hardly the call to action that can inspire and motivate underachieving blacks to improve their lives. Instead, it further demoralizes those poor blacks who are doing the best to keep their children and themselves out of harm's way, often against towering odds, while still being hammered for their alleged failures by the Cosbys within and without their communities. Worse, Cosby's blame-the-victim slam does nothing to encourage government officials and business leaders to provide greater resources and opportunities to aid those blacks that need help.
>
> *Come on People*, intended or not, continues to tar the black communities and the black poor as dysfunctional, chronic whiners, and eternally searching for a government hand-out. Come on, Cosby.[7]

The criticism of Cosby presents an interesting dilemma: how do you regard those who are living with these difficulties? Is it possible to be a critic of Cosby while also resisting the temptation to identify blacks primarily as victims? It seems that even while acknowledging

---

[7]Earl Ofari Hutchinson, "Come on People, No, Come on Cosby," *The Huffington Post*, October 18, 2007; http://www.huffingtonpost.com/earl-ofari-hutchinson/come-on-people-no-come-on_b_68990.html (accessed April 29, 2010).

there is a place for responsible action (none of the critics deny this), the critical responses direct our focus to some form of perpetual victim status. What path can we take to find an identity beyond this label?

WHO TELLS THE STORY?

In the late 1980s I once had a dream in which Spike Lee came to me and asked, "What does it mean to be black?" I don't think I gave an answer before I woke up, but I remember being disturbed by this question that assumed the existence of an "authentic" black identity. In answering this chapter's question about identity, it is important to briefly draw attention to the effort made to strengthen the African-American community by overcoming the false identity formation that results from the legacy of racism. While there may be some broad agreement that the history of slavery and Jim Crow in the United States devastated and enslaved the minds of many African-Americans, there are different approaches to healing, uncovering, or creating a proper identity. Perhaps one of the most significant strategies has been to discover the "true" history of African-Americans as a remedy. Eddie Glaude refers to this as the "archaeological approach" in which "black identity is concerned with uncovering our true selves and inferring from that discovery what we must do. Black identity is interpreted here in terms of reality and appearance. There is a *real* way of being black and a *false* way. Something out there is essentially black, and when we lose our way, as some of us have because of white supremacy, we need only find 'it' and all will be well."[8] One might say that the aim of the approach is to replace a false narrative (given by the oppressor) with the true one (uncovered and passed on by those who have learned about, for example, our true African selves). The idea is that an authentic story will yield authentic practices and facilitate liberation.

This archaeological approach locates identity in a cultural retrieval project. This strategy may have some relevance, but it

---

[8]Eddie S. Glaude Jr., *In a Shade of Blue: Pragmatism and the Politics of Black America* (Chicago: The University of Chicago Press, 2007), 53.

relies upon the idea of an authentic ancient history that all African-Americans must know in order to be properly self-actualized. It also seems to run the risk of trading one dominant narrative for another, with the notable exception that the storytellers are no longer white oppressors. Correcting the lies of a white supremacist narrative is a genuine moral obligation, but is it enough to replace the lies with some version of another cultural history? How do we affirm our cultural uniqueness and our common humanity and resist the siren song that would exalt essential or ontological blackness as the answer to the norms of whiteness? Our cultural stories alone will not suffice. A theological vision can help us have a deeper sense of identity that incorporates the gifts of our culture without requiring us to go on an expedition for a mythical conception of blackness.

WHAT DOES GOD SAY?

The Bible tells the story of our salvation. In this story God reveals our identity. The term *story* does not mean myth or fable but reflects the fact that there is an overarching narrative (some use the term *metanarrative*) in Scripture from which doctrines emerge that should inform the way we view ourselves. Creation, fall, redemption, and renewal are vital categories/doctrines for understanding who we are and how we should live. If we desire to understand our plight as humans as well as the promise that catalyzes a hopeful existence, then we should put our specific focus on theological anthropology, which answers the question, what does it mean to be human? The four categories/doctrines can be seen as four chapters of the story, with each providing vital content perspective as we attempt to solve the riddle of our identity. It is very important to consider all four of these chapters; in answering this anthropological question, we discover our ultimate purpose, which in turn helps frame our approach to life, whether our circumstances are favorable or otherwise. A partial answer is more detrimental than helpful because it fails to truthfully show how God's revelation addresses the plight of those who could easily see themselves as victims.

Creation. Genesis 1–2 gives us two complementary perspectives on God's creation. Regarding the creation of humans, Genesis 1 emphasizes that the one true God has created human beings in the divine image. While some draw a distinction between the words "image" and "likeness" in Genesis 1:26, it is likely that they refer to the same idea. For example, Genesis 1:27 uses "image" alone, and later Genesis 5:1 uses "likeness" alone, and both texts are expressing the same meaning respectively.[9] Genesis 2 brings a sharper focus to the making of the first person and to the specific responsibilities given to humans as the stewards of God's creation.[10] As beings created in the image of God, humans are distinct from the rest of the created order and the only ones who are made to be like God in certain ways. In light of the concerns of this chapter, there are some important implications of humans as divine image bearers. First, it is important to recognize that the biblical text makes no reference to skin color. While this may seem obvious, this is important because the significance of being human has nothing to do with the percentage of melanin in one's skin. While the Bible later acknowledges differences in appearance, it does not link the value of persons with their skin tone. Humans as divine image bearers have in common a shared dignity that is based in God's pronouncement that "it was very good" (Genesis 1:31).[11] God calls the entire creation good, and that includes humans. This truth is echoed in Psalm 8:5–6:

> Yet you have made him [man] a little lower than the heavenly beings
> and crowned him with glory and honor.
> You have given him dominion over the works of your hands;
> you have put all things under his feet.

All humans are crowned with a glory and honor bestowed upon them by God, and they also have the tremendous privilege of caring for the entire creation. This great task of creation stewardship is

---

[9]See Anthony A. Hoekema, *Created in God's Image* (Grand Rapids, MI: Eerdmans, 1986), 13.
[10]An interesting book specifically focused on this is Anthony J. Headley, *Created for Responsibility* (Anderson, IN: Bristol House, 2006).
[11]Given our culture of superlatives, "very good" should be understood in its best sense as excellence, or as many would say today, awesome.

given as a functional expression of humanity created in the divine image. Some call this the cultural mandate or creation mandate. This mandate is an expression of God's desire that the entire creation flourish. Genesis 1:26 states this dominion over creation as part of God's creational intent, and Genesis 1:28 presents this great responsibility as a command given to our first parents. Why is this important? There are two points to make here. First, the responsibility for the entire created order implicitly means that humans have the responsibility to seek the flourishing of other human beings, the very crown of creation. This mandate compels us to seek the best for everyone. Second, responsible participation in God's world is central to our purpose as human beings. One constant emphasis in *Come On People* is the need for blacks to act responsibly. What is the most fundamental reason why anyone should act responsibly? Is it because of our parents or our community or our loyalty to some group? I suggest that all of these reasons should be subordinate to the recognition of our creational purpose. God created humans to be responsible people, bestowed with an inherent dignity. How much does the frame of creation influence our concepts of responsibility?

Fall. Unfortunately, the story does not end with creation. While we are given dignity and purpose as divine image bearers, the story takes a horrific turn. In Genesis 3 the first sin occurs, and all of us have been victims ever since. Though it is still God's good creation, the fall introduces massive distortions. Four relationships are altered as humans are fractured internally and have breaches with God and the created order and enmity with other humans. As a result of sin, the divine image is altered in a way analogous to a cracked mirror or like the hall of mirrors in a carnival funhouse. Humans retain the image of God but fail to consistently or properly express any likeness to the Creator. The fall leads to a change in our natures. We are prone to act sinfully; it is difficult for humans to act in ways that seek the flourishing of others and to express love to others in selfless ways. In contrast, the responsibility given to humans becomes twisted. Power is often used in oppressive ways, and some apathetically disregard the various kinds of stewardship necessary for a flourishing creation. Some want to control everything, some want to fight, others want to give up, and some are simply apathetic.

Fallenness makes distortion "normal" and leads us to see ourselves and others in incomplete and false ways. It is as if we make our home in a hall of mirrors and base our perception on the ubiquitous warped reflections. We struggle to understand and appreciate the dignity that God has given to all of us, but instead we typically regard ourselves either too high or too low. Sometimes we make those "like us" into objects of worship and "others" into objects of disdain. In other instances we loathe ourselves and make others into idols. We humans range about like sheep who do not know who they are or whom they should follow. If we take the effects of Genesis 3 seriously, it should not be a surprise that a general glance at human history or a specific focus like that in *Come On People* shows us many ways that things have gone wrong for our race. The carnage and subsequent reverberations of white supremacy are but one example of the cycles of oppression and victimization that go back as far as Cain's murder of Abel. Post-fall reality is often a living hell.

Redemption. If the Fall were the final word, then *victim* is the proper label for every human (even the ones who don't know it as they bask in self-worship). Genesis 3:15 promised that the Serpent's head would be crushed one day by the Messiah. Even though human history moved forward with consistent expressions of sinful distortion, God promised that one day the world would be set right. God told Abraham, "In you all the families of the earth shall be blessed" (Genesis 12:3). This blessing began to come to fruition with Jesus, the divine-human Son of God who at the beginning of His ministry announced the advent of God's kingdom (Mark 1:15). The good news of the gospel is that through Christ the ruptures of the fall will be healed. Here is a place where we must be careful because it is important to convey that the gospel is not merely a spiritual pacifier that comforts us in the face of difficult challenges. In terms of identity specifically, the good news of the gospel is that our full humanity is given back to us in Christ. Christ, who is the fullness of the divine image, not only demonstrates a completely human existence but sends the Spirit to believers to not only make us alive to God but also capable of living in accordance with the creational intent. This is not immediately complete transformation but a process in which we "have put on the new self, which is being renewed in knowledge after the image of its creator" (Colossians 3:10). When we talk about being "saved," we are speaking of the reconciliation we have with God through justification, but also much more. We are participants in a process of sanctification that is not only concerned with our internal holiness but also with our private and public practices that spring from obedience to the cultural mandate and the first and second greatest commandments (Matthew 22:37–40 tells us that all the commandments are expressions of our love for God and neighbor). Redemption is the good news that we are God's children, members of His family who model the realities of God's kingdom wherever we find ourselves.

What does this mean for the challenges that concern Cosby and Poussaint? First, it means that we can never see ourselves as victims if we see our true humanity through the lens of the gospel. The story of redemption must counter the multiple narratives that emerge from the legacy of racism, corrosive media, and the desperation on display in poor communities. We acknowledge the reality of fallenness but move beyond that to practices empowered by hope. Second, it is important to emphasize the path to improvement as an expression of sanctification. God's transforming work through the Spirit enables Christians to live as kingdom witnesses. This includes attending to the needs of the most downtrodden but also stewarding our personal agency in efforts to improve our own circumstances. As Christians we are kingdom citizens who celebrate our common humanity and praise God for the richness of our diversity as creatures; we can praise God for our ethnic/racial particularity without the need to deify our culture.

Renewal. Eschatology is the end of the story, when God will bring all things under the reign of Christ. While there is often a focus on the debates related to the final sequence of events (tribulation, rapture, millennium, etc.), it is also important to consider how eschatology can inform our identity. If we think of eschatology as the final culmination of redemption, we can also think of it as the full restoration and fulfillment of our humanity. Humans rightly related to God through Christ will become the realization of God's original intent in creation. For the present time this becomes a source of hope that is based on Christ's resurrection and anticipated return. We live in an "already, but not yet" kingdom that Christ inaugurated when he conquered death: "And he is the head of the body, the church. He is the beginning, the firstborn from the dead, that in everything he might be preeminent" (Colossians 1:18). Our hope in the future directs our gaze to a day when we are free from our personal, relational, and societal dysfunction. An eschatological vision tells us where we are going. In the words of the band King's X, "we are finding who we are," an echo of 1 John 3:2: "Beloved, we are God's children now, and what we will be has not yet appeared; but we know that when he appears we shall be like him, because we shall see him as he is." We will continue to discover the profound truth of our God-given identity until the final day. This perspective helps us resist any sense that current circumstances are final and reminds us that God is in control of history. God will change us and will transform the world into the kingdom. The promise of our future humanity gives us hope while we practice sanctification expressed as faithful responsibility to ourselves and for our communities. As dire as some of the crises above appear, we press forward in light of an assured victory. Eschatology at its best is far from "pie in the sky" theology that leads us to escape. Instead our vision is set on what we will become and where we are going. At the end we will be made perfect in God's image.

A PLEA FOR CATECHESIS

God's story of salvation should be prominent and foundational in the identity formation of Christians. The great problems identified by Cosby and Poussaint will not be sufficiently addressed if we seek our identity and best practices in our cultural uniqueness or if we are so terrorized by the magnitude of the crises that we can only lament our status as victims. We should also remember that while these great problems present themselves intensely in the black community, these problems are not only ours; these challenges are present throughout the human race in ways both similar and distinct. The path forward must include the church as a context for identity formation. How do we do this? There are many strategies that we can take, such as the recently proposed Male Investment Plan (MIP) that emerged from "The Gathering" in March 2010. Over six thousand people from the three African-American Methodist denominations (A.M.E., C.M.E., and A.M.E. Zion) met in Columbia, South Carolina, to address the crisis with African-American males. Bishop John R. Bryant states that the MIP will "focus on spiritual enrichment, mentoring, education, economics, health and wellness, prevention of imprisonment and job preparation. We will also seek advice from our churches and community partners across the country, which have been actively engaged in male mentorship and male strengthening programs. And we are still listening to God, who will shepherd us through a process we are confident will change lives."[12] This is an encouraging multifaceted effort that offers a lot of promise.

I would like to offer another suggestion based on the educational function of the church. One of the best things churches can do is to develop a range of ways to teach their people biblical and theological truth. Preaching, Bible study, Sunday school, and special seminars or classes are opportunities for practicing what the ancient church called catechesis ("teaching"). The purpose of catechesis is

---

[12]Bishop John R. Bryant, "AME Church: Help All Families by Helping Black Men," *The Washington Post*, April 5, 2010; http://newsweek.washingtonpost.com/onfaith/guest voices/2010/04/ame_church_help_all_families_by_helping_black_men.html (accessed April 30, 2010). Also see http://www.greatgathering.org/.

to educate those who enter the church so that they understand what it means to be part of God's people. How many people who occupy pews on Sunday understand what God says about their identity? The church plays a role in identity formation, but to what degree? What message is conveyed?

It is vital to examine the curriculum that we are using and to consider how we can make sure that identity formation occurs when people become church members. Admittedly we are in an attention-challenged society where the idea of teaching church doctrine in a classroom format can be very challenging. This does not mean abandoning the direct oral communication of biblical and doctrinal content, but it is important to recognize that learning happens in a number of ways. Catechesis does not need to be limited to the verbal transmission of information; churches can brainstorm and devise ways to convey the content of the faith linked to concrete expression of our responsibility as humans. For example, if church members participate in planting gardens in their neighborhoods, commit to cleaning up entire street blocks or initiate tutoring programs in educationally challenged areas, they are exhibiting a central aspect of their identity as those created in God's image. Another idea could be encouraging those with an interest in media to write and stage one-act plays or short video clips that present different images than those that are marketed in Hollywood films and music videos. One great aspect of these activities is that they can also engage the community not only as an evangelistic witness but also as a message that tells those outside the church that God cares for them. If these kinds of activities are not simply fun church programs but are part of the process of bringing people into the church, they can begin to see their identity as image bearers who are being renewed in their minds and deeds. Conveying doctrine does not need to be an arid experience but can be practically linked to everyday life. Creative catechesis can immerse church members in the biblical narrative that informs and empowers them to live a victorious life that contributes to the flourishing of God's creation.

The way of the good and blessed life is to be found entirely in the true religion wherein one God is worshipped and acknowledged with purest piety to be the beginning of all existing things, originating, perfecting, and containing the universe. Thus it becomes easy to detect the error of the peoples who have preferred to worship many gods rather than the true God and Lord of all things, because their wise men whom they call philosophers used to have schools in disagreement one with another, while all made common use of the temples.

AUGUSTINE, *On True Religion*, i.1[1]

Keep your child in the schools, even if you have to eat less, drink less and wear coarser raiments; though you eat but two meals a day, purchase but one change of garment during the year, and relinquish all the luxuries of which we are so fond, but which are as injurious to health and long life as they are pleasing to the taste.

BISHOP DANIEL ALEXANDER PAYNE,
Welcome to the Ransomed[2]

Nothing hinders the perception of truth more than a life devoted to lusts, and the false images of sensible things, derived from the sensible world and impressed on us by the agency of the body, which beget various opinions and errors.

AUGUSTINE, *On True Religion*, iii.3[3]

---

[1]Quoted in J.H.S. Burleigh, *Augustine: Earlier Writings* (Philadelphia: Westminster Press, 1953), 225.
[2]Quoted in Milton C. Sernett, ed. *African American Religious History: A Documentary Witness* (Durham, NC: Duke University Press, 2001), 235.
[3]Burleigh, *Augustine: Earlier Writings*, 226.

2

THE BLACK FAMILY: THE HOPE OF "TRUE RELIGION"

Bruce Fields

Cosby and Poussaint, on the one hand, laud the opportunities for success that exist in the United States despite the legacy of racism that still influences the present, recognizing, on the other hand, many harmful behaviors that many black youths still take up for various reasons. They do identify, however, "an important element" that contributes to this troublesome situation:

> We feel that an important element in this crisis is the breakdown in good parenting. We're not telling you something you don't know. In too many black neighborhoods, adults are giving up their main responsibility to look after their children. In all corners of America, too many children are getting the short end of the stick as extended family networks collapse and community support programs fail to replace them in any significant way.[4]

My purpose in this piece is to reflect briefly on matters that will strengthen the black family and facilitate the emergence of a greater number of black youths who will help lead this nation to even greater days ahead.

A legitimate inquiry can be made: Why would anyone concerned about the contemporary black family begin with quotes from Augustine? The relevance of the second quote above can be

---

[4]Bill Cosby and Alvin F. Poussaint, MD, *Come On People: On the Path from Victims to Victors* (Nashville: Thomas Nelson, 2007), 57.

more immediately appreciated, but nevertheless I will respond to the question with three propositions that I hope will motivate a fresh consideration of the relevance of these quotations for any doubters. I want to demonstrate that the wisdom of the ancient, corporate church is still applicable today, even for the black family.

First, my reflection is aimed primarily at the church of Jesus Christ, comprised of those who have put their faith in Him alone as their atoning sacrifice for the forgiveness of sin and reconciliation with God (Romans 5:10–11). Augustine has been an influential theologian and philosopher in the church, with elements of his thought being embraced by much of Christendom since his death in A.D. 430. This North African bishop was, however, simply a church-man who attempted to minister to his flock through the multiple aspects of his ministry. In short, he was a pastor who was concerned about the life and thought of that segment of the church entrusted to his care. The church has selectively embraced its past in the search for instruction and wisdom, and Augustine is an authoritative con-tributor to this search.

Second, Augustine taught not only from Scripture and church tradition but also from his own life's lessons. An immediate con-nection between his life and the issues of this piece is his family life. Things were not very smooth in his household or in his life in gen-eral. He struggled with his father (Confessions 1.11.17)[5] and had a periodically strained relationship with his mother (Confessions 5.8.15). He had a son born out of wedlock, Adeodatus, a gifted young man who died at an early age (Confessions 9.6.14). At one point he put aside his son's mother to position himself for a mar-riage that would advance him socially while holding the position of chief rhetorician in Milan (Confessions 6.15.25). At a pivotal time God got ahold of him (Confessions 8.12.29) and enabled him to be a grace-empowered minister who could speak biblically to many important matters. The foundational truth that Augustine embraced more and more in the course of his life was that the only stable thing

---

[5]All citations come from The Confessions, trans. Maria Boulding (Hyde Park, NY: New City Press, 1997).

in life is the Lord Himself. Life can have much uncontrolled variability, but God remains who He is and what He is about.

This leads to my third proposition. Augustine contributes to the wisdom of the church and to the wisdom needed for the benefit of the black family with his emphasis on the pursuit of true religion as the proper orientation for all aspects of life. This orientation is good for the church in general, but it is also the hope, specifically, for the black family. To flesh out this concept for the sake of greater applicability, I will need to explain it in a manner sufficiently nuanced for it to speak to the hope of the black family.

True religion is the pursuit of the one true God. This pursuit tests the nature of all things in life and shapes all visions and goals in life. The church is to be a sign and model of this pursuit. The black family, understood through the lenses of the Scriptures and the church, should be also a sign and model of this pursuit. Despite the horrors of slavery, Jim Crow segregation laws, and the present, pervasive effects of racism and poverty, the family has survived and does survive. The foundations for the perpetuation of the family and the enhancement of its effectiveness in the African-American community must incorporate some historical reflections, beginning with an analysis of the devastating effects that slavery had on the black family in America.

Slavery created a situation of profound dehumanization demonstrated in numerous ways but concretely shown in the lack of integrity present in slave marriages and child-rearing.[6] Families could be easily broken up, with family members being sold simply at the master's whim or because of economic necessities. The Jim Crow era allowed some advancement for the African-American community, but its humiliating effects had economic ramifications because there were fewer opportunities for jobs. Recently racism has taken the form of disparate advantages for members of the dominant white culture compared to those given to blacks.

During the 1960s Great Society initiative, Daniel Patrick

---

[6]E. Franklin Frazier and C. Erick Lincoln, *The Negro Church in America/The Black Church Since Frazier* (New York: Schocken, 1974), 37–40.

Moynihan advanced the controversial case that other factors besides racism were harming the African-American community.[7] The problem was essentially the embrace of a culture that denigrated marriage, creating environments where many children were being raised in single-parent families, a potentially harmful situation in which children were often growing up without the regular presence of fathers. This enhanced not only the number of births out of wedlock but also raised the percentage of people living in poverty. Moynihan and his cohorts were accused of racism and insensitivity to other key factors affecting the black community, but his findings have been affirmed in recent times.

Despite its good intentions, the Great Society's war on poverty hurt the black family in the long run. The original intent of the program was admirable. President Lyndon Baines Johnson (1908–1973) described the Great Society as "a place where men are more concerned with the quality of their lives than the quantity of their goods."[8] As an extension of the program and in response to a number of riots taking place in Harlem (1964), Newark (1967), and Detroit (1967), culminating in the assassination of Dr. Martin Luther King Jr. (1968), Johnson appointed the Kerner Commission (National Advisory Commission on Civil Disorders) to investigate the causes of such unrest. The commission concluded, "Chronic poverty is a breeder of chronic chaos."[9] Eliminating poverty, it was believed, would eventually bring about the elimination of the frustration and rage that bred chaos. Giving blacks, particularly black males, jobs would enhance the stability of the black family.

The Great Society had noble goals. Many involved in the formulation and implementation of the program wanted "abundance and liberty for all, an end to poverty, an end to racial injustice."[10]

---

[7]"The Negro Family: The Case for National Action," *The Moynihan Report (1965)*, Office of Policy Planning and Research, United States Department of Labor, March 1965; http://blackpast.org/?q=primary/moynihan-report-1965 (accessed November 10, 2010).
[8]Cited in Stanley K. Schultz, *American History 102, Civil War to the Present*, Lecture 27: "The Almost Great Society: The 1960s"; http://us.history.wisc.edu/hist102/lectures/lecture27.html (accessed January 14, 2009).
[9]Ibid.
[10]The Economic Opportunity Act of 1964 included such initiatives as Head Start, Job Corps, work-study programs for university students, VISTA (Volunteers in Service to America), Neighborhood

But harmful developments in the black family began to emerge, despite good intentions and government "equalization" programs. Kay S. Hymowitz observed that the Johnson administration initially embraced the findings of the Moynihan report. The administration, however, also distanced itself from it based upon charges of racism in the report as well as pressure from feminist critics who viewed the two-parent family as the "oppressive ideal of the nuclear family. . . . Convinced that marriage was the main arena of male privilege, feminists projected onto the struggling single mother an image of the 'strong black woman' who had always had to work and who was 'superior in terms of [her] ability to function healthily in the world.'"[11] Hymowitz concludes with a statistic also found in Cosby/Poussaint's book: "70 percent of black children are still born to unmarried mothers."[12] Poverty and the perpetuation of poverty in subsequent generations is often due to joblessness, but in many situations fatherless families also cause it.

A sociocultural analysis of this breakdown in familial relationships can often lead to discussions about the effects of poverty, joblessness, and the lack of the sacrifices needed to build and maintain a family. These sacrifices, for example, take the forms of commitment to one's spouse even in tough times, learning to control one's

---

Youth Corps, basic education and adult job training, and CAPS (Community Action Programs), ibid.

[11]Kay S. Hymowitz, "The Black Family: 40 Years of Lies," *City Journal* (Summer 2005); http://www.city-journal.org/printable.php?id=1824 (accessed September 22, 2008).

[12]Ibid. See also Cosby and Poussaint, *Come On People*, 14. Hymowitz constructed a telling summary:

> So, have we reached the end of the Moynihan report saga? That would be vastly overstating matters. Remember: *70 percent of black children are still born to unmarried mothers* [emphasis hers]. After all that ghetto dwellers have been through, why are so many people still unwilling to call this the calamity it is? Both NOW and the National Association of Social Workers continue to see marriage as a potential source of female oppression. The Children's Defense Fund still won't touch the subject. Hip-hop culture glamorizes ghetto life: " . . . 'cause nowadays it's like a badge of honor / to be a baby mama' go the words to the current hit 'Baby Mama,' which young ghetto mothers view as their anthem. Seriously complicating the issue is the push for gay marriage, which dismissed the formula 'children growing up with their own married parents' as a form of discrimination. And then there is the American penchant for to-each-his-own libertarianism. In opinion polls, a substantial majority of young people say that having a child outside of marriage is okay—though, judging from their behavior, they seem to mean it's okay, not for them, but for other people. Middle- and upper-middle-class Americans act as if they know that marriage provides a structure that protects children's development. If only they were willing to admit it to their fellow citizens.

emotions for the family's well-being, and postponing the fulfillment of desires for the good of the family. From a biblical/theological perspective, I believe that the Great Society invited a radical departure from a focus and dependence upon God and His ways for solutions to the problems facing blacks in America. The embrace of the Great Society was essentially the movement from dependence on the one true God to dependence on the human institution of government. This is a theological assessment of a historical, economic, sociocultural phenomenon. Such programs may indeed take on concrete sociocultural, political, and economic forms, while still being oriented in ways that reflect the acknowledgment of and respect for God. The church is the community that should primarily reflect this perspective, the orientation that I see as the continuation of true religion.

Because of God and His ways, any solutions that only involve governmental programming and do not intentionally protect and preserve the black family are doomed to failure. I will attempt a survey of biblical and theological considerations to advance the case for such protection and preservation. The first part will examine some biblical passages that reflect the importance of honoring marriage. Admittedly, I will not be able to address all relevant biblical material, but some foundational passages will be identified. The second part will engage some theological categories and propose the implications they have for the black family. Through such reflections I will attempt to explicate the meaning of "true religion," particularly as it relates to pursuing a life before God that provides an orientation and evaluation of all areas of life, including the life of the family.

BIBLICAL AND THEOLOGICAL REFLECTIONS

The instructive contributions of specific passages fit into a biblical story line. That story line is made up of many people, sub-stories, and teachings, but many would agree that the overarching story line is the story of God's redemptive plan for humanity and creation

(Romans 8:22–25). The pivotal figure for the accomplishment of this redemption is Jesus Christ. The view of marriage, including its meaning and its significance, is an essential part of this story line. My purpose is to show that the biblical view of marriage is portrayed against the backdrop of God's redemptive plan. When appropriately oriented in God's plan, a person, a couple, or a people are about the business of practicing true religion.

I will be looking at a few texts from Genesis, Deuteronomy, Proverbs, and the Gospels. Many others could be cited, but my intention is simply to demonstrate the type of biblical narrative where marriage is portrayed.

Genesis

Genesis 1:26–27 speaks of God creating humanity ("male and female," 1:27) in His image. The passage entails many possible meanings of "image" that cannot be fully discussed here. It will suffice to incorporate a couple of observations. Millard Erickson summates the meaning of the image as "the elements in the human makeup that enable the fulfillment of human destiny. The image is the powers of personality that make humans, like God, beings capable of interacting with other persons, of thinking and reflecting, and of willing freely."[13] Charles Sherlock correctly observes that the text does not tell us specifically what the image is, rather, we are told what it "*involves*: living in a series of relationships."[14] The capacity to form relationships creates the elements for the institution of marriage (Genesis 2:24–25). God brings it about and facilitates a bond with a deep, profound nature. The relationship between Adam and Eve produces children with both a troublesome (Cain: 4:1, 8) and a more positive (Abel: 4:2, 4) nature.

God's concern for the integrity of marriage is shown early to His special servant, Abram. It is through His servant that God reveals His concern to others. In Genesis 12:15–16 Pharaoh takes Sarai into his household because Abram had previously lied and said that

---

[13]Millard J. Erickson, *Christian Theology*, second edition (Grand Rapids, MI: Baker, 1998), 532.
[14]Charles Sherlock, *The Doctrine of Humanity* (Downers Grove, IL: InterVarsity, 1996), 37.

Sarai was his sister, leading Pharaoh to believe that she was "available." Genesis 12:17 speaks of the Lord's afflicting Pharaoh and his household with diseases because he had taken Sarai, Abram's wife, as his own, albeit unknowingly. Pharaoh then confronts Abram with his lie (12:18). Elements of God's overarching plan had to be fulfilled (12:1–3; 15:4), and part of that fulfillment was the protection of Abram and Sarai's marriage.

Much of the rest of Genesis records relationships where a number of the patriarchs had multiple wives or relationships that produced a child (Abraham, Genesis 16; Jacob, Genesis 29–30). Concurrently, however, is the presence of multiple references to a singular "wife" in the narratives, suggesting a foundational relationship. I will identify a few examples. Genesis 12:5 reads, "And Abram took Sarai *his wife*" (emphasis mine). Abraham (formerly known as Abram until God changed his name) forbade the eldest of his servants to find a wife for Isaac among the Canaanites, but in Genesis 24:4 he commanded him to "go to my country and to my kindred, and take *a wife* for my son Isaac" (emphasis mine). Jacob had sons by his wives Leah and Rachel and by their maidservants, Zilpah and Bilhah, respectively (later described as "wives," Genesis 30:9; 30:4). Nevertheless, after Isaac blessed Jacob, he commanded him:

> Arise, go to Paddan-aram to the house of Bethuel your mother's father, and take as *your wife* from there *one* of the daughters of Laban your mother's brother. (Genesis 28:2, emphasis mine)

There are other such references in Genesis. These are mentioned to show that even though many men took more than one wife, it seems that "one" was elevated to a status above the other wives. In the example of Abram, this is undoubtedly a demonstration of the sanctity of the marriage relationship. The sanctity of marriage between a man and a woman is more clearly demonstrated in Deuteronomy.

Deuteronomy

Deuteronomy gives a great deal of attention to the covenant that God established with the people of Israel. Within the context of the reaffirmation of the covenant (Deuteronomy 5:2ff.), Moses reestablishes the authority of the Ten Commandments. Two of them have specific application to the protection of marriage, while a third assumes a one-to-one correspondence in a marriage relationship. The fifth commandment, "Honor your father and your mother, as the LORD your God commanded you, that your days may be long, and that it may go well with you in the land that the LORD your God is giving you" (5:16), suggests marriage is a relationship between *two* individuals. J. G. McConville observes:

> The Fifth Commandment moves into the realm of the social order. Respect for parents includes the obedience of children, the most obvious modern inference from this command. In Israel, however, the requirement of obedience lasted beyond childhood, to the point where young people had to answer for their failings in this regard before the representatives of the whole community (Deut. 21:18–21).[15]

This concept's application to the contemporary scene can be illustrated through a lament from Cosby and Poussaint. They remind the reader of earlier days when if one was tempted to do something foolish, like stealing, one always considered how that action would reflect on your parents. "If you get caught stealing it, you're going to embarrass your mother . . . You're going to embarrass your family."[16] They lament that such a perspective is not as pervasive in the African-American community as it once was.

The seventh and tenth commandments show a more immediate burden to protect the marriage relationship: "You shall not commit adultery" (5:18), along with, "You shall not covet your neighbor's *wife*. And you shall not desire your neighbor's house, his field, or his male servant, or his female servant, his ox, or his donkey, or

---

[15]J. G. McConville, *Deuteronomy* (Downers Grove, IL: InterVarsity, 2002), 128.
[16]Cosby and Poussaint, *Come On People*, 2.

anything that is your neighbor's" (5:21, emphasis mine). Adultery is understood typically as parties engaging in actions or levels of relationship only appropriate within a marriage relationship with people outside of their current marriage. It can be more easily understood as unfaithfulness to one's marriage vows.

Much could be said about Deuteronomy 24:1–4 if I was discussing the matter of divorce,[17] but 24:5 contributes to understanding a healthy marriage. The Jews allowed young couples to have some time free from normal responsibilities, with hope that a foundation would be built that would help avoid potential negative developments down the road. McConville observes that there was also an economic incentive to allow this stretch of freedom from normal responsibilities: "Behind the hope of a happy marriage, there were also economic tensions that might arise on the death of a young man who was childless."[18] This was a social, cultural, and political environment that encouraged the protection of marriage in a unique way. The word of the Lord commanded it. It was recognized that marriage was a foundational part of society. It still is.

Many more implications addressing the ideal nature of marriage could be drawn from Deuteronomy and other sections of the Old Testament. Nevertheless, I will have to limit the rest of my observations to a primary representative of the wisdom literature, Proverbs. As in the previous sections, I am not attempting an exhaustive study of all relevant material. I will be content to continue a demonstration of how the story line of Scripture, though its overarching theme is God's redemptive plan, nevertheless reveals insight about God's perspective on marriage. These insights give more concreteness to the possibility of living in the realm of true religion.

Proverbs

Proverbs speaks often of "the fear of the LORD" (1:7). This "fear" is a profound reverence for God and is supposed to be the organizing principle for all aspects of life. This organizing principle is summa-

---

[17]See, for example, McConville's treatment, *Deuteronomy*, 357–60.
[18]Ibid., 360.

rized in Proverbs 3:5–6: "Trust in the LORD with all your heart, and do not lean on your own understanding. *In all your ways* acknowledge him, and he will make straight your paths" (emphasis mine). This is the proverbial equivalent to Augustine's concept of "true religion." One of the areas that Proverbs addresses throughout the book, which is fundamental to a proper life before God, is marriage and family. If applied specifically to the black family, the family is strengthened and prospers when it models and sustains life in "the fear of the LORD" or in the realm of "true religion." Proverbs reveals the wisdom and necessity of protecting the husband/wife relationship, while also providing guidelines for a healthy life for the members of a family.

First, much in terms of this protection focuses on staying away from the adulterous person. The frequency of such concern is a demonstration of God's desire to protect life in general (7:7, "a young man lacking sense")[19] but specifically to protect marriage (2:16–17; 5:3–14, 20). Second, there is a great deal of blessing to be had when the covenant-marriage relationship is respected. The teacher encourages a husband to "rejoice in the wife of your youth" (5:18; see 5:15–19). Many other exhortations could be identified, but one that has particular meaning to me is 19:14: "House and wealth are inherited from fathers, but a prudent wife is from the LORD." The epitome of a wise woman is described in Proverbs 31:10–31.

Finally, I will mention a few examples of family life as portrayed in the book of Proverbs. Parents are admonished to raise up a child "*according to his way*" (22:6, emphasis mine).[20] Though there must be consistent principles that parents should enforce consistently with all their children, there must be an accompanying awareness of the disposition of each child. It sometimes takes a bit more prayerful effort to train a child with a respect for how he or she processes and responds to the parents' consistently held principles. Discipline of a

---

[19]Another helpful section in this regard is Proverbs 6:27–35. There can be legitimate, harsh consequences when a man becomes involved with another man's wife.

[20]The ESV rendering of Proverbs 22:6 is, "Train up a child in the way he should go; even when he is old he will not depart from it." I am following the lead here of John W. Miller, *Proverbs* (Scottsdale, PA: Herald Press, 2004), 159–160.

non-abusive sort helps instill such principles in the deep recesses of the child's soul. Coupled with this are the commands that the child should listen to his/her parents. For example, Proverbs 6:20–21 encourages such commitment: "My son, keep your father's commandment, and forsake not your mother's teaching. Bind them on your heart always; tie them around your neck." The commandments, of course, are assumed to be reflective of God's revealed directives. If a child wishes to honor his/her parents and give them joy in life, the child should pursue a pathway of wisdom (10:1; 13:1; 15:20). "Shame and reproach" come to one who does "violence to his father and chases away his mother" (19:26; cf. 20:20).

At no time have all of God's commandments been obeyed, but the Scriptures do provide ideals to pursue. History, as well as the contemporary environment, shows that abuse can run rampant in families, and the Scriptures recognize this by guarding against it. My point is that living in "the fear of the LORD" still requires an advocacy and protection of marriage and the family. I will explore only one passage from the Gospel of Matthew to show the Lord Jesus' concern for marriage. Again others could be discussed, but Matthew 19:3–9 is pivotal for a number of reasons.

Matthew 19:3–9

> And I say to you: whoever divorces his wife, except for sexual immorality, and marries another, commits adultery. (Matthew 19:9)

My point in reflecting on this passage is to counter any interpretation of this text that entertains a clear, surefire case for divorce. There are simply more factors to consider. The Lord Jesus Himself was an advocate for the protection of marriage. He was also one who insisted on the practice of children honoring their parents.[21] Marriage was to be intensely protected because of the command of

---

[21]Jesus accused the Pharisees and scribes of "break[ing] the commandment of God for the sake of [their] tradition" (Matthew 15:3). They could withhold aid to their parents by declaring something as a "gift" to God. Jesus held them accountable because "tradition" presented them the opportunity to disobey the Lord.

God, in part because so much could be determined about the orientation of a people before God by what they thought and practiced about marriage.

This section in Matthew follows a passage dealing with the magnitude of God's forgiveness and the call for others to forgive similarly (18:21–35). The Pharisees tried to draw Jesus into a debate on the proper interpretation of Deuteronomy 24, which was the basis for the different opinions on divorce represented by the schools of Hillel and Shammai.[22] Jesus bypassed the whole discussion by appealing to what God intended for marriage from the beginning. He combined, in Matthew 19:4–5, references to Genesis 1:27 and 2:24 and then emphasized two fundamental understandings regarding marriage in 19:6. First, he said, "They are no longer two but one flesh." Keener suggests that the force of "one flesh" is "the language of family ties and alliances (as in 2 Sam 5:1)."[23] Second, in the same verse there are the accompanying words, "What therefore God has joined together, let not man separate." Marriage is something with which God is intimately involved. Thus from a biblical narrative perspective marriage is far more than a mere sociocultural institution.

Of course, if one denies the authority of Scripture, this would affect one's view of marriage. Another consideration for the rejecters, however, is to reflect on the question, why is it that in societies where marriage and family relationships are in widespread disarray, the society does not maintain its identity and power much longer in comparison with the length of time it may have been in existence?

The meaning of 19:9 must also be understood in relation to the question Jesus was asked regarding why Moses allowed a certificate of divorce (19:7). He confronted the Pharisees with the fact, "Because of your hardness of heart Moses allowed you to divorce your wives" (v. 8). It is very important that we consider the rest of the verse: "but from the beginning it was not so." Jesus would

---

[22]See specifics on this discussion in Craig S. Keener, *Matthew* (Downers Grove, IL: InterVarsity, 1997), 295.
[23]Ibid., 295.

again bring them back to God's original intent reflected in Genesis. The exception, then, for divorce in 19:9 is for "sexual immorality" (porneia). This word can have a broad range of meanings: fornication, adultery, something indecent.[24] To come to a proper conclusion on the significance of this passage, we must consider a bottom line—marriages without some practice of forgiveness will not last. The force of the passage is more geared toward one who has a long, unrepentant involvement with sexual immorality. This then in a very real way can be considered a fundamental violation of the covenant/marriage relationship.

The biblical-redemptive story line demonstrates that God intends to guard the perpetuation of marriage. Admittedly, many more passages could have been studied, but I believe these are sufficient to establish this perspective as the biblical one. What happens in the family greatly influences other familial and societal developments.

Much could be said about such developments through sociocultural and economic lenses. For example, young people can learn about the importance of education from their life in a family. This would enable them to engage and assist society, where there is an inherent interdependence among members. They could learn about the importance of courtesy and respect for people in general, especially for the elderly and for those who have achieved great things through hard work and sacrifice. An ideal would be learning the importance of honest, skill-building work. I hope that through various forms of modeling, a young person can learn that there is much to be gained by maintaining faithfulness in all aspects of work. I am old enough to insist that young people in the African-American community learn that it is a privilege and a responsibility to vote.

Nevertheless, I also want to offer some needed reflection about the theological teaching that could take place within a context of solid marital relationships where there is a strong desire for the well-being of children.

---

[24]See an extended treatment in D. A. Carson, Matthew (Grand Rapids, MI: Zondervan, 1995). 413–18.

Some Theological Categories

These will not be extensive treatments, but I wanted to entertain some possibly valuable lessons that could be learned through the family, particularly believing families, by reflecting on doctrines related to God, Christ, and the church/community.

Children process various impressions and understandings about God that they encounter early in their family life. Is God near? Does God comfort and protect? Is God reliable? What does it mean that "God is love" (1 John 4:8)? What does it mean to refer to God as "our Father" (Matthew 6:9)? These questions only illustrate the types of developments that can take place in the mind of a child. These developments can have great effect upon subsequent learning and understanding. Having said this, I would admit that I have personally struggled with my own understanding of God because my father was not as present in my childhood as he should have been.

The long and short of it is that through the grace of God I determined that my children were going to know who their father was, whether they liked it or not. I had begun to understand that the development of their personal faith would be greatly affected by what they saw in me, as well as by what they saw in their mother and in my relationship with her. I have sometimes communicated to our children that they are the "fruit" of our love. Their mother and I are one couple, though we are each a distinct person. We are one family, yet each of the members is a distinct and precious person. This is not an attempt to draw an exact correspondence with the doctrine of the Trinity, but such a balance of relationships can build a unique understanding of individuality, leading to an enhanced ability to understand the Trinity. The appropriate conception is to view oneself not as an autonomous self but as both an individual and a member of a family. This can contribute greatly to building identity and establishing a sense of belonging.

The doctrine of Christ traditionally consists of a study of both the person and the work of Christ (the meaning and significance of the atonement). Though numerous observations and applications can be made in this area, I will offer only one observation on His atonement that can provide a helpful lesson that can be effectively internalized in a family setting.

The apostle Paul writes in 1 Corinthians 15:3 that "Christ died for our sins in accordance with the Scriptures." In Philippians 2:5 he begins a pivotal passage on the person and work of Christ: "Have this mind among yourselves, which is yours in Christ Jesus." Paul then speaks of Christ's radical obedience, submitting to death to accomplish the Father's will. The principle seen here is that meaning in life often involves some elements of self-sacrifice. This means focusing on others and their needs rather than on your own. Teaching children to consider how their actions affect others and to always consider the consequences of an action will be very beneficial to their development into responsible adults. Much can be accomplished when Jesus is set forth as the example for our life and the Holy Spirit is acknowledged as the power behind our life (Ephesians 5:18). With concrete examples and the empowerment that God makes available through the Holy Spirit, a young person can consistently practice the type of sacrificial spirit that Christ displayed on Calvary.

CRITICAL TEACHING AND APPLICATION FOR THE CHURCH

The church must continually focus on a multifaceted response to the challenges facing the black family. In terms of an overarching theme, the church should actualize a teaching-preaching-modeling strategy that places the divine institution of marriage within the context of God's redemptive plan. Pastors and church leaders must teach the biblical story, keeping the climactic figure of Jesus Christ in the forefront. An essential and fundamental part of the biblical story is God's view of marriage and what it takes to build a family. In terms of true religion—seeking the Lord and living appropriately before Him—the family, along with the church, must model and perpetuate this perspective. I will offer some generalized suggestions on how

The Black Family   57

the church can be a more effective servant in bringing greater health to the black family.[25]

Witnessing to the Gospel

All that I have said thus far about what is needed for the health of the black family and the black community in general is futile apart from the transformative power of the gospel of Jesus Christ. The church must continually witness to humanity's need for the forgiveness of sin and reconciliation to God that is only available through faith in Jesus Christ. The apostle Paul writes in Romans 5:10–11:

> For if while we were enemies we were reconciled to God by the death of his Son, much more, now that we are reconciled, shall we be saved by his life. More than that, we also rejoice in God through our Lord Jesus Christ, through whom we have now received reconciliation.

Humanity's greatest need is to be reconciled to God. This insistence, admittedly, may lack sociocultural, economic, political, and historical sophistication, but it is the foundation for all hope (Colossians 1:27). Elsewhere the apostle speaks of the reality of empowerment. In 1 Corinthians 2:3–4 Paul talks about his "weakness," "fear," and "much trembling" in the fulfillment of his ministerial responsibilities, but his hope is in the power of the Spirit. So it is possible to speak of principles and strategies that would be beneficial for the life of the black family, but the power needed to fulfill said principles is another matter. True religion begins with a living, vital relationship with God through faith in the Lord Jesus Christ.

Centers for Study, Sharing, and Prayer

The formal aspects of the church, in terms of Sunday school and the various worship services, are indeed important. Another level

---

[25]For greater attention to a specific training program, see: Dr. Willie Richardson, *Reclaiming the Urban Family: How to Mobilize the Church as a Family Training Center* (Grand Rapids, MI: Zondervan, 1996).

of aid can be applied effectively at the lay level. I refer to centers, but this simply means small groups giving attention to Bible studies and mutual counseling. This level of interaction and accountability is crucial. Pastors and pastoral staff teams cannot cover all the needs of a congregation. There is a level of vulnerability and encouragement that can take place only in small groups. The church should identify lay leaders who are able and willing to open up their homes for these types of engagements. Prayer practiced in these kinds of settings facilitates comfort and accomplishes much (James 5:16).

Reconciliatory Liturgy

Pain, misunderstandings, and divisions happen in families. The church can do much to strengthen families through teaching on the blessings of good communication and forgiveness. People have to communicate with one another to have to hope of maintaining healthy relationships. The church should aid the development of such conversations. Reconciliation is best achieved when there is acknowledgment of wrongs (confession) and the asking of forgiveness for whatever one has done to contribute to pain and division. There may even be a need for some sort of ceremony to seal the meaning and significance of what has transpired to the people involved. Though I am sure that some churches already practice such reconciliatory liturgy, perhaps there could be a libation or some symbolic passing of an object that brings to mind the meaning of the forgiveness and reconciliation that has occurred. It may be ideal to have witnesses to hold the parties accountable through prayer and to observe the responsible parties' future behavior. They promise to each other that they will move beyond the painful events that transpired in the past in order to experience the healing and peace of reconciliation. With these proposed guidelines I am assuming that the family members involved are believers in the Lord Jesus Christ. Reconciliation with God and the power of the Holy Spirit are required for the effectiveness of such liturgy.

Outreach to the Surrounding Community

The church prepares itself for outreach by following through on the suggestions above. Modeling is so important for service to the community. A concrete way of engaging the community regarding marriage and family is to provide lay listeners. This does not require formal training, though that would be helpful. This involves having laypeople who are able and willing to listen and pray with people in the neighborhood who need someone to talk to. So much in terms of witness and modeling can take place at this level.

Because of the dangers of abuse in the family, some people advocate offering alternative structures for relationships, projecting more "open" understandings and greater toleration for less than the biblical ideal. For the black family, however, our recent history has demonstrated that such a view has been devastating to the community. Evidences have pointed to this fact, but there are those who benefit politically and economically from such devastation. Because of this, poor family habits and practices will still occur, and listeners will still be needed. They will occupy the place of spokesperson. They will be needed to take care of the masses from the storehouse of their compassion.

Marriage and family life must be conducted in the context of Augustine's understanding of "true religion," pursuit of the true knowledge of God and His ways. Many elements of life are changeable and beyond personal control. Yet in the flow of true religion, there will emerge not only instruction but also encouragement, comfort, and power. It would seem that a concern for what transpires in marriage and family is one that is widespread. It is something that goes beyond race, culture, even geography. The following quote from a Native American holy woman reflects this transcendent concern:

> It is very important that your girls and young men become purified through the sacred rites of the Sacred Pipe, for they are bearers of the new life and they form the families that must walk in the sacred way in order to surround their children with wisdom,

honor, goodness, and purity. In the family, the husband and wife should become one in thought and deed and one also with the Great Spirit. *But if they turn their thoughts from the holy way and think with desire for the bodies of others, then they destroy themselves with self and passions, and deprive their children of the Sacred Water of the Spirit. From such families come the ones who harm the world.*[26] (emphasis mine)

---

[26]White Buffalo Calf Maiden, in Vinson Brown, *Voices of Earth and Sky: Vision Search of the Native Americans* (Happy Camp, CA: Naturegraph Publishers, 1976).

3

SEXUALITY IN THE BLACK COMMUNITY

Howard Brown

In this chapter we will consider sexuality and the black community, a sensitive but crucial subject.

THE PLACE OUR SEXUALITY BEGAN

The Bible begins with a creation story in which God created man and woman and made them naked, but in that nakedness they were unashamed. In other words, they were known, could know each other, and could know God in their nakedness. They were not afraid to be touched and seen by each other. No dangerous or deceitful motives or covert agendas existed. Adam and Eve's full frontal, physical, uncovered presentation said with sensual candor, "This is who I am." What they saw in the beauty and the acts done in the body perfectly reflected the souls wonderfully encased within them. That raw, uncensored, benevolent ability and exercise to know, be known, and explore one another is called intimacy. Human sexuality, in terms of sexual intercourse and interactions between men and women, is only one God-given way to express physical intimacy.

The story of Adam and Eve goes on to tell us that humankind broke away from God and in doing so became a broken creation. Having lost the *full* ability and desire to reflect the image of God and relate intimately with God, humanity literally sought to cover its losses. This cover-up dimmed the light of their knowledge about themselves and each other. Intimacy—naked freedom and benevolence toward one another—suffered. Shame, fear, hatred, and destructive behavior remained, now hindering and harming the intimacy necessary to be sexually whole. At the same time, we continue to harbor a God-given, yet broken desire and drive to be intimate sexual creations. Our intimate longings hobble along, leaving a jagged, damaged path of broken relationships in their wake.

Although damaged, our sexuality continues to make us "naked." It lays bare much of what is right and wrong on the inside. It expresses who we really are and what we really feel. At the same time, it opens us up to experience and exposes all sorts of internal, invisible damage. Our sexuality and its behavior mirror the condition of our souls and the souls of our community.

This is no different for black people. Our sexuality reveals our humanity. The expressed result of that sexuality confirms that black people, along with other human beings, are beautiful but broken. The cultural peculiarities of black sexuality, seen in ethnic statistical data and exploited on the stage of popular culture, provide an important picture of the souls of black people. What does this tell us?

THE PLACE OF SEXUAL BROKENNESS

In *Come On People*, Bill Cosby and Alvin Poussaint highlight many concerns about broken black sexuality. Among them are the number of single mothers, absent and apathetic fathers, the lack of two-parent homes, teenage pregnancy, and the spread of STDs. The statistics accompanying their comments are somewhat alarming:

> According to 2007 Census Bureau data, 34 percent of black families with children under eighteen years old are homes led by single mothers compared to 9.5 percent for whites.[1]

> According to 1997 data, African-Americans comprise about 27% of young teenage mothers [editor's note: this was down 42% from

---

[1]Bobbi Bowman, "The (Poor) State of Families," *The Root*, http://www.theroot.com/views/poor-state-black-families (accessed March 18, 2011).

1991]. Nevertheless, factoring in the fact that African Americans make up a smaller percentage of the U.S. population, the rate of black teenage pregnancy is very high. Looking more closely at African-American teens aged 15–19, the rate is almost double that of the white population.[2]

The prevalence of STDs among blacks is startling. According to 2009 Centers for Disease Control figures, blacks accounted for 71 percent of all gonorrhea cases in 2009, though they represent 14 percent of the U.S. population. In fact, the gonorrhea rate among blacks is twenty times higher than whites. Blacks represented almost half of all reported chlamydia cases (48 percent), which is eight times higher than rates for whites. Blacks also accounted for 52 percent of all syphilis cases in 2009, which is nine times higher than the white population.[3]

Minority women constitute only about 13% of the female population (age 15–44) in the United States, but they underwent approximately 36% of the abortions . . . black women are more than 5 times as likely as white women to have an abortion.[4]

That means that, on average, about 1,800 black babies are aborted daily.

In the timely words of Cosby, come on, people! It is time to examine seriously the results of our sexual behavior and what it reveals about us. Obviously we are a passionate people, hungry to be known and to know each other. We have the potential to achieve a high degree of fulfilling relationships. Unfortunately, it seems that we are only having a lot of sex. These statistics show that many of us are behaving like a shell of a people and have disconnected our sexuality from our God-given sense of worth and intimacy.

God created black people, along with all human beings, to fulfill their humanness. Any failure of intimacy in our sexuality

---

[2]"Bill Cosby Sets the Record Straight on African American Teen Pregnancy," July 20, 2004; http://www.news-medical.net/?id=3210.
[3]"Trends in Sexually Transmitted Diseases in the United States: 2009 National Data for Gonorrhea, Chlamydia, and Syphilis," Centers for Disease Control, http://www.cdc.gov/nchhstp/newsroom/docs/2009STDSurvReportMediaFactSheet.pdf (accessed March 18, 2011).
[4]"Abortion and the Black Community"; http://www.blackgenocide.org/black.html.

short-circuits our emotional and relational processes. Judging by its product, our sexual behavior (the manifestation of our sexuality) declares that we are broken. Clearly this failure is an internal malfunction of the soul and heart. But how did this happen?

THE PLACE OF FAMILY IN OUR SEXUALITY

As Cosby and Poussaint state, the family is central to understanding and moving toward sexual dignity as a people, because the family shapes our sense of sexuality and our understanding of its proper expression. God created human beings to influence each other. This means we are responsible for shaping each other. Genesis says that God brought Eve to Adam (Genesis 2:22). Then Adam blessed her, declaring to her, to the world, and to himself that she was a dignified bearer of God's image. By declaring, "This at last is bone of my bones and flesh of my flesh; she shall be called Woman, because she was taken out of Man" (v. 23), Adam announced that Eve shared in the same essence of humanity that God had created in Adam. What was "this" became "Woman" through the infusion of God's created image. God later ratified this blessing by calling Adam and Eve to be fruitful and multiply. They were to pass on who they were, based on who God had made them—examples of healthy relationships between men and women. God made it this way so we would learn how to properly approach and express sexuality, dignity, and intimacy as passed down from our elders, parents, and community; and He made it this way so we would learn by word and by deed.

THE PLACE OF MARRIAGE IN OUR SEXUALITY

If men and women are not present, active, and engaging in committed, rightly intimate relationships with each other, sexual mess occurs. As Adam proclaims, the marriage between our original parents refers to a psychosomatic unity.

> Therefore a man shall leave his father and his mother and hold fast to his wife, and they shall become one flesh. (Genesis 2:24)

"One flesh" refers to a spiritual unity between the man and the woman. Adam declares just as much about the soul of Eve as about her body. Their sexuality functions properly only if they are socially, emotionally, and spiritually one. If the latter fails, so will the former. In *Othello* Shakespeare refers to the sexual act as "making the beast with two backs."[5] Marriage makes one beast out of two distinct creatures, man and woman. Their sexuality is the physical expression of that "beast." No wonder sex malfunctions outside of marriage! No wonder a lack of committed relationships brings so much pain and struggle! We cannot live the lie of having sexual wholeness outside the sanctity of marriage. Our sexuality problems are also our marriage problems, and we have passed them on to the next generation. Below is an excerpt from a writer who in 2006 visited a sixth-grade class in Washington, DC, for a career exploration:

"Marriage is for white people."

That is what one of my students told me some years back when I taught a career exploration class for sixth-graders at an elementary school in Southeast Washington. I was pleasantly surprised when the boys in the class stated that being a good father was a very important goal to them, more meaningful than making money or having a fancy title.

"That's wonderful!" I told my class. "I think I'll invite some couples in to talk about being married and rearing children."

"Oh, no," objected one student. "We're not interested in the part about marriage. Only about how to be good fathers."

And that is when the other boy chimed in, speaking as if the words left a nasty taste in his mouth: "Marriage is for white people."

He is right, at least statistically. The marriage rate for African Americans has been dropping since the 1960s, and today, we have the lowest marriage rate of any racial group in the United States. In 2001, according to the U.S. Census, 43.3 percent of black men and 41.9 percent of black women in America had never been married, in contrast to 27.4 percent and 20.7 percent respectively for whites. African American women are the least likely in our

---

[5]William Shakespeare, *Othello*, in *The Literature Network*, 1604; http://www.online-literature.com/shakespeare/othello/2/.

society to marry. In the period between 1970 and 2001, the overall marriage rate in the United States declined by 17 percent; but for blacks, it fell by 34 percent.[6]

A number of really difficult and heartbreaking reasons exist for the decline of marriage in our community. It can feel more freeing to leave behind, or let go of, what for many has become the disappointing institution of marriage. Our people resort to what I would describe as a neo-nihilism that masquerades as freedom but is really a loss of hope. In a world that remains disappointing and hard, God calls us to live and be healthy. We must dig for and ask the Lord for ways to redeem what He has created as good for us but has been destroyed and demeaned by so many.

All said, I must take a step back and confess: I do not believe marriage, in and of itself, is the answer to our sexual brokenness. Marriage itself can be only as healthy as the people it unites. I agree with Bell Hooks, in part, as she discusses what she describes as an "idealized fantasy" presented by shows like *The Cosby Show*:

> . . . if there was a man in the house, a father, everything would be perfect; they would be happy. . . . When black pundits, whether political figures or intellectuals, talk about the black family, they too seem to buy into the romantic myth that if only there was a black man in the house, life would be perfect. Like children, who know better, they refuse to accept the evidence that there are plenty of homes where fathers are present, fathers who are so busy acting out, being controlling, being abusive, that home is hell and children in those homes spend lots of time wishing the father would go away. . . . Dysfunctional homes where there is no love, where mother and father are present but abusive are just as damaging as dysfunctional single-parent homes.[7]

Hooks rightfully asserts that even in a context of marriage, damage occurs. Marriage alone cannot shoulder the entire burden

---

[6]Joy Jones, "Marriage Is For White People," March 26, 2006; http://www.washingtonpost.com/wp-dyn/content/article/2006/03/25/AR2006032500029.html.
[7]Bell Hooks, *We Real Cool: Black Men and Masculinity* (New York: Routledge, 2004), 102.

of our sexual dysfunction. At the same time, we must resist the temptation to dismiss it as merely beneficial to our sexuality. It is where our sexuality begins and departs. If intimacy between a man and a woman forms the core of the sexual act, a departure from the God-given context of psychosomatic unity will only compound the damage of our sexual brokenness. If marriage becomes the exception instead of the norm, we are doomed to sexual weariness. Marriage defines the sexual act and sets its stage and scope. Marriage frees intimacy to convey dignity and worth. Marriage says, "You are my destination." Without the commitment and sanctity of marriage, intimacy can never fully manifest itself, and we will be disconnected and disoriented in our intimacy and sexuality. We will then pass this distance and disconnection on to our children.

THE PLACE OF BROKEN RELATIONSHIPS IN OUR SEXUALITY

So we must ask ourselves, what does the sexual act become outside of a context of intimacy and commitment? Before Adam and Eve ate from the tree of the knowledge of good and evil, they were "naked and . . . not ashamed" (Genesis 2:25). They did not fear exploring and being explored by each other. Adam and Eve were not afraid that they would use that unguarded existence to hurt, take advantage of, or abuse each other. Their differences did not make them insecure; their differences connected them to each other. However, when Adam and Eve sinned against their Creator, they lost their sense of worth, respect, and trust for God. This meant they also lost their sense of worth, respect, and trust for themselves and each other.

> So when the woman saw that the tree was good for food, and that it was a delight to the eyes, and that the tree was to be desired to make one wise, she took of its fruit and ate, and she also gave some to her husband who was with her, and he ate. Then the eyes of both were opened, and they knew that they were naked. And they sewed fig leaves together and made themselves loincloths. (Genesis 3:6–7)

Out of the desire for something other than God's provision, Adam and Eve not only sold out on God, they failed to protect and cover each other. Eve fed the forbidden fruit to Adam, and Adam, who was with her, failed to stop her from being seduced by the Serpent's lies. They both traded their nakedness for security in their own wisdom. From that point on, human beings could no longer trust that they would not be used, overlooked, and unprotected in their nakedness. According to the Scriptures, we fear intimacy with others because we are open to all sorts of abuses. The fall caused the first humans to break their proper relationship to everything and everyone around them. Shame has entered each one of us. We covered our nakedness and our newfound guilt and fear with fig leaves that did not work. Adam and Eve covered themselves from each other and their God. They now viewed their sense of intimacy and their freedom to know each other with fear and distrust. They were ashamed of their dispensability, frailty, and culpability. Intimacy became dangerous, and when intimacy is dangerous, we want to be divorced from it. Without true intimacy, sex is nothing more than a cheap counterfeit. On one hand, because sex is intimate by its very nature, we use it as a cover-up and a healing agent to provide some of the intimacy that we once had. On the other hand, because we are divorced from the true intimacy Adam and Eve knew before the fall, and because we share their fear of nakedness, we also use sex as a tool of violence, rage, and control.

In their chapter on "What's Going on with Black Men," Cosby and Poussaint state:

The fact is, though, that many of the black females who used to get married when they became pregnant are no longer doing so. There is less shame and less embarrassment.[8] . . . Not long ago a television show featured a thirteen-year-old mother who had somehow managed to have two of her suitors appear on the show for a paternity test. One of the boys was black, the other Puerto Rican. They were fifteen- and sixteen-year-old best friends, who

[8]Bill Cosby and Alvin F. Poussaint, MD, *Come On People: On the Path from Victims to Victors* (Nashville: Thomas Nelson, 2007), 14.

both had had sex with this young girl during the general time she conceived. The word *shameless* comes to mind. Why these people would wash linen this dirty not just in public but on national TV is still another sign that all is not well in the world.[9]

I agree with Cosby/Poussaint that these examples are a sign that all is not well in the world, but I do not agree that shamelessness or a lack of shame is the problem. I believe it is shame exactly that has driven these people to seek an antidote for their brokenness. Sometimes the antidote looks and feels like justice and being known and respected (opposites of shame) when it is actually another way of responding to the shame of their insecurity, abandonment, and disgrace. Shameless behavior is an outward cry of the inner rage and sorrow of a person whose humanness is unmet, untouched, and unknown. They rightly feel sold out, used, and desperate enough to display humiliation in order to reclaim the sexual dignity that has escaped them.

THE PLACE OF MEN IN OUR SEXUALITY

Our people, especially our men, are hiding something and hiding from something based on the issues of our sexuality. Cosby/Poussaint state:

> The more socially impotent the black man is feeling, the more he will rely on sexual conquests to prove his manliness. There's a lot of bragging among black men when sex and paternity are the main claims to fame. Some will see getting a girl pregnant and having a child as proof of their virility. But what it really proves is their insecurity.[10] . . . Real men act responsibly, and they sure as hell don't walk away from the mothers of their babies. Real men make a commitment to these young mothers. If they do not marry them, at least they should take care of their children.[11]

Black men are having a hard time being "real men" as Cosby/

---

[9]Ibid., 15.
[10]Ibid., 13.
[11]Ibid., 14.

Poussaint describe them because many are running and are hiding from what responsible manhood will be sure to reveal—their lack of "manliness." Black men suffer from being boys who cannot handle the internal rigors and demands of committed relationships and adult responsibilities. They refuse to grow up because they fear being weighed, measured, and found wanting. Our men wrongly believe sexual acts will cover and remove the pain of not feeling man enough in a fallen world. They are tempted to try to outrun the overbearing weight of their sexual and relational responsibilities. "Hit it and quit it" becomes the *modus operandi* of the black man who is afraid to be found emotionally and financially incapable of being a "real man."

Cosby/Poussaint write:

> . . . Some black women simply don't want to marry the fathers of their babies because these men appear to have little to offer beyond sperm. Many of these men are unemployed and unemployable.[12]
> . . . Because so many black men are unemployed, underemployed, and incarcerated, they are not proposing marriage and if they did, their proposals might not be taken seriously. A father takes care of his children. These men have trouble taking care of themselves. The relationship between them and the mothers of their babies is often strained, or worse.[13]

If a black man's worth hinges upon his ability to provide financially, he will run away from his responsibilities in shame. Though provision is not, and should not be, excluded as one of the dignifying attributes of manhood, provision is not, and should not be, exclusive or premier among them. If it is made an issue between him, his woman, and his child, a black man, or any man for that matter, will malfunction. Those who should be the object of his affection and attract his sacrificial attention simply become reminders and aggravations of his failure. Bell Hooks writes:

---

[12]Ibid.
[13]Ibid., 15.

Most black males have consistently received contradictory messages from society about what it means to be responsible. Patriarchal socialization says you are responsible if you get a job, bring your wages home, and provide for your family's material well-being. Yet poverty and a lack of job opportunities have prevented many black males from being responsible in the patriarchal sense of the term. Many black males accept this definition of responsible manhood and spend their lives feeling like a failure, feeling as though their self-esteem is assaulted and assailed on all sides, because they cannot acquire the means to fulfill this role.[14]

Out of sheer rage and anger toward the women who appear to rob their sense of worth, some men become vigilantes of lost manhood by conquering women sexually. They wrongly seek justice for what they deem unjust and unfair measurements of their manhood by being sexual Robin Hoods. Most men, in their bragging, boasting, and violent objectifying behavior, are seeking to conquer and defend in what seems to be a war against their manhood. Tragically, this means men will demean, depress, and destroy their familial responsibilities in an attempt to remove their condemning presence over them. This can lead a man to enter the same type of irresponsible relationships and to father more children, continuing in a lifestyle that will only increase his sense of shame.

If he will not wage war against what serves as a mirror to his weaknesses, he will simply run away and hide from his shame. He will turn away from his woman and children altogether, disowning them as not just irrelevant to his manhood but malevolent. Therefore, children and mothers may not see the father for days, months, or years, and in extreme cases the father may disappear from their lives forever.

Some men have abandoned being in sexual relationships with women at all, turning to homosexuality as a safe haven from the constant reminders of their lack of true manliness. It can be more comforting and safe to take on an effeminate persona, especially if

---

[14]Hooks, *We Real Cool*, 85–86.

they think being a man in the wake of failure is too difficult and too disgracing.

Men are hiding from and warring against the condemnation and exposure of their broken and fallen manhood. Let us look back at the account in Genesis:

> And he [Adam] said, "I heard the sound of you in the garden, and I was afraid, because I was naked, and I hid myself." He [God] said, "Who told you that you were naked? Have you eaten of the tree of which I commanded you not to eat?" The man said, "The woman whom you gave to be with me, she gave me fruit of the tree, and I ate." Then the LORD God said to the woman, "What is this that you have done?" The woman said, "The serpent deceived me, and I ate." (Genesis 3:10–13)

All men shield and cover their nakedness and their exposure to guilt and condemnation from their women and children. Man seeks to escape facing himself, God, and his responsibilities because he does not have an answer for his internal or external corruption. Women have responded to this neglect with equal anger and apathy.

THE PLACE OF WOMEN IN OUR SEXUALITY

Women, rightly offended by the often-abusing sexuality of black men, turn to protective mechanisms too. A black man who walks out on her and her children is a constant reminder that she is not worth the effort or the attention. Black men have succeeded in their passive and active sexualized aggression. The black woman is theirs to be sexually conquered and impregnated, and that is it. Our women, wanting to be touched and known, even if falsely, will fold to this pressure. Some women actually believe having sex with uncommitted men means they are loved. This creates a sexualized intimacy between a man and a woman. They both seek to answer their deep longings with superficial sexuality. They fool themselves into thinking that this will satisfy their longings to be known, cherished, and encouraged. In the end, both people feel the letdown of sex that is handled like a drug—it only temporarily masks the symptoms of an unmet, deeper desire for intimacy. Women, as do men, easily turn to sexually addictive and foolish behaviors in a failed attempt at wholeness.

In a sexualized intimate relationship, it is easy for a woman to see the child created in the process as the emblem of worth and value after the man has abandoned the relationship. Motherhood becomes a way of keeping her dignity and grace intact. She was not good enough to be someone's wife or, if married, an emotionally cared for wife, but she does have a consolation prize—her children. Thus the cycle continues for her and her children. Black community leaders have rightly focused on drug addiction and abuse as a source of many problems within the black community but have failed to focus on the consequences of sexual addiction and abuse on our people and their sense of dignity.

This can happen to the married or the unmarried. In many marriages sex is divorced from intimacy. The husband and wife stay married out of convenience, shame, or to sustain their fantasy of being good people.

Nevertheless, both men and women participate in the dance. Like a man who runs away out of shame, a woman may refuse to invite her man to anything higher or better as far as intimacy is concerned. If she has already felt like a sexual object, conquest, or prescription, she will protect what is left of her on the inside. She will not be vulnerable with the man or demand that he become a better man because his potential failure is too great a risk. She will seek to protect herself by being strong, living life on her own, and raising children by herself. She will take control of her sexual life by enjoying her sexuality as objectively as the men around her enjoy it, or she may turn to the comfort and safety of a same-sex relationship; she will not allow her heartfelt desire for deeper respect from men to surface. To do so would open her up to more pain and stigmatize her as being overly demanding. In that way she allows the man to maintain his behavior as they both behave as wary, jaded consumers of each other.

Only after the high of having sex, being in a fake relationship, or having a child wears off will a woman's own sense of rage surface. However, that often perpetuates the problem. She will rage against the father of the child or blame the child as the remnant of a disgracing experience with a man. She may be tempted to use the child to cover her shame and exact justice against the cavalier and disappointing father. She can do this by not allowing the father to see the child or to be in the child's life. An emotionally abandoned mother, single or married, may use the man as a scapegoat for all that has gone wrong, indoctrinating her children and other young women along the way. She may even transfer her unmet longings to the child, forcing a young boy to become mama's protector or the new man of the house or her counselor or a sounding board for her grown-up issues. Sometimes these children witness their mother's lonely and empty sexual pursuits with man after man. The mother is trying to stay alive emotionally, but like a drowning victim grabbing for life, she may drown her children with her in her sexual brokenness. No wonder young girls can grow up believing that a man is good for babies and sex but bad for long-term emotional relationships.

THE PLACE OF CHILDREN IN OUR SEXUALITY

In his book *Silently Seduced: When Parents Make Their Children Partners*, Dr. Kenneth Adams describes what he coins as "covert incest" in contrast to the physically abusive overt incest:

> Covert incest occurs when a child becomes the object of a parent's affection, love, passion, and preoccupation. The parent, motivated by the loneliness and emptiness created by a chronically troubled marriage or relationship, makes the child a surrogate partner. The boundary between caring and incestuous love is crossed when the relationship with the child exists to meet the needs of the parents rather than those of the child.[15]

---

[15]Kenneth Adams, *Silently Seduced: When Parents Make Their Children Partners* (Deerfield Beach, FL: Health Communications, 1991), 9.

Adams goes on to describe covert incest in many ways—as a child becomes mama's "prince," mama's "confidant and advisor," or mama's "little man." However, no matter the profiles, the violation and abuse complicates mothers' sexual lives. This abusive pattern, so common in the black community between mothers and sons, ironically often makes the boys into womanizers. Their womanizing covers the shame and anger of unhealthy relationships with their mothers. They seek justice and freedom from the abuse—either by never entering into a meaningful relationship with a woman outside of the sexual act or by becoming Casanovas who, like little boys with an adult sexual drive, seek to "comfort" all the emotionally distressed women in their lives. Worse, some become straight objectifying misogynists who are sexually addicted and driven to have sex with as many women as they can demean. These men are ashamed, angry, and empty. They do not allow themselves to condemn the only person who seemed to love them; they do not acknowledge their emotionally stunting, shaming abuse. Thus the downward spiral continues.

However, this "covert incest" is not exclusive to mothers. Father-to-son sexual abuse and overt incest occurs often in the black community. It occurs when black men brag about their sexual conquests to pubescent and prepubescent boys incapable of committed emotional relationships with women. These boys observe crass, even pornographic descriptions of male exploits. The mere discussion of such things with adolescent, teenage, or younger boys is a form of sexual abuse, causing much of the same damage as physical sexual abuse. The images, deposited by men they trust, rip their way into the tender psyche of our boys, leaving deep scars that surface in their later sexuality. Compounding the problem is the belief that these misogynistic exploits and portrayal of women affirm their entry into manhood. In other words, boys face rejection and shame from men, whose respect and love they want to gain, unless they participate in this emotionally disconnected and sexually broken lifestyle. If they do not, they are derided and demeaned. No wonder so many brothers are on the "down low." They are running away from abuse, seeking unconditional love from men who will not belittle and shame them. Boys grow into men who want relief from the traumatic teaching that sexual exploits are a rite of passage. This leads to the same downward spiral as these men are confused and frightened by anything that is more than just sex.

As bell hooks writes:

> Many womanizing black males have experienced traumatic sexual abuse in childhood. It scars them for life. And when they receive the message from the culture that real men should be able to endure abuse as a rite of passage and emerge with their sexual agency intact, there is no cultural space for them to articulate that they were sexually abused, that they are damaged and in need of sexual healing.[16]

As black men and women, we bear the scars of this abuse and neglect. Unless we are touched, known, healed, and forgiven, we will live according to the longings, emptiness, and offense of that neglect and abuse.

As we discussed earlier, God created humans with an ability to pass on our sense of worth. This is not completely good news according to what we have discovered thus far. This means that married or not, if our parents are not healthy sexually, we probably will not be either. If our parents do not have nurturing relationships, we will not. If our parents treat each other with derision, we will do the same. Married or not, parents play a central role in developing and contributing to the ethos of our children's sexuality. Malfunctioning sexuality stems from a shared lack of worth passed on to us by our parents, particularly our fathers.

If parents are emotionally and sexually anemic, their children will grow up to be emotionally adolescent adults who struggle with a profound and deep appetite for unmet intimacy. Unfortunately for many, sexualized intimacy becomes the "food" of choice. Confused

---

[16]hooks, We Real Cool, 80.

and heart-hungry men and women feast on each other sexually in a futile attempt to fill the void. This hungry emptiness is an epidemic among our black men and women who have become, and are creating yet another generation of, sexual addicts and deviants. But is there hope? Is there help? Is there a place of healing and sexual wholeness? Indeed there is.

THE PLACE OF REDEEMED SEXUALITY

Extreme pain and death mark the road to this place. Facing and realizing the abandonment, abuse, and neglect caused by our sexual brokenness, while necessary for rehabilitation, overwhelms the sinner. Who can or wants to hear and face all of that condemning truth? Some of these issues will take more than one lifetime to fully change as we continue to walk and live in present ruins.

Cosby and Poussaint wisely look at and point us to education, advances in civil rights, and better health care as being helpful in dealing with the symptoms of our sexual brokenness. As a pastor, I propose that we have one more place to explore.

Cosby characterized many of our churches as clouded and represented by leaders and institutions more committed to being economically successful than spiritually relevant. Nevertheless, in the message of the Bible, the gospel, there is still a place.

After Adam and Eve sought to control their sense of worth, which separated them from God's dignity and shackled them with sin-laden shame, God called them out and back to Him.

> And they heard the sound of the LORD God walking in the garden in the cool of the day, and the man and his wife hid themselves from the presence of the LORD God among the trees of the garden. But the LORD God called to the man and said to him, "Where are you?" (Genesis 3:8–9)

Like Adam and Eve that day, living and crouching in fear and disgrace, the best words for our black men, women, and children to hear from God are, "Where are you?" In this profound question

God invades our world of hiding and covering and calls us together before Him to face what we would not and could not face on our own—our sin. God calls us to examine and confront the mishandling and abuse of others and ourselves. He calls us to a place where we can look squarely at ourselves and see our failure. In addition, as God turns us around to face our self-destruction, He also turns us to face Him, a position that allows Him to heal our hurt. Though intimacy has escaped us in many ways, God does not let His broken people escape Him. God promises to recognize black people; He does not ignore or reject His own.

Moreover, God delivers on His promise. Though like Adam and Eve we bear the just effects of our sexual sin, God does not seek to shame or condemn us. He lovingly calls broken people to approach Him for healing and redemption.

> And the LORD God made for Adam and for his wife garments of skins and clothed them. (Genesis 3:21)

God brings His people to a place where they can be redeemed from their sexual sins. Though often skewed by malpractice, the church remains the place where broken people can find refuge, where we, both the sexually offensive and the offended, can be unashamedly known and invested in without fear of condemnation. The church, the people God has called to Himself, remains the place where we practice the message of God's transforming grace in healing our sexual sin. In this place people provide each other with counseling, confrontation, and reconciliation. In this place we call men to see and be seen by their Creator in ways powerfully intimate enough to call them out of a fallen image of sexuality into God-ordained manhood. In this place women can hear the words of God that pronounce they are God's beautiful creation. This place is a clinic—a spiritually therapeutic place that redeems the emotional, social, and mental souls of people. But this community is a place of healing because a person of healing is central to it.

We know how great an impact (albeit in this discussion, damaging) a mother, father, boyfriend, or girlfriend can have on our progeny and on us. Just imagine if there were a new Adam. Imagine if there were a new source of our humanity that could have just as great an impact as Adam and Eve's on our sexual lives. Without a new Adam redemption could not occur, and the world would continue to bear the brokenness caused by Adam's sin. But God has provided a new Adam to heal our sexual brokenness. God sent someone to be intimate with us and to meet us in our shameful condition. God sent someone who feels all that we feel in our sexual pain and yet does not let it make Him hate, despise, use, or condemn us. He works and speaks transforming life to us. When God spoke judgment to the Serpent that misled our first parents, he said the following:

> I will put enmity between you and the woman,
>   and between your offspring and her offspring;
> he shall bruise your head,
>   and you shall bruise his heel. (Genesis 3:15)

The offspring of the woman is the second Adam, the intimate knower of our condition, the Lord Jesus Christ. What this Scripture tells us is that He would be born into our sin, into the broken sexual experience and heritage of black people, but would not let it remove Him from us. He will not let it keep us from true and lasting dignity, if we only choose to follow Him. He is promising to restore and redeem us. He will do this by becoming the power and hope that guides our pursuit of sexual wholeness through education, health reform, and civil rights. He has come to create a place of forgiveness, confession, and courageous disclosure of our sexual dysfunction, a place without shame and with real hope that we will be made right through Him.

Come on, people! I know a place where redemption and healthy sexuality can be found.

As if poor black kids didn't have trouble enough, they often turn
to these rappers, even the gangsters, as role models.

BILL COSBY AND ALVIN F. POUSSAINT
(Come On People: On the Path from Victims to Victors)

If I act like a pimp ain't nothin' to it gangsta rap made
    me do it
If I call you a nappy headed ho ain't nothin' to it gangsta rap
    made me do it
If I shoot up your college ain't nothin' to it gangsta rap made
    me do it
If I rob you of knowledge ain't nothin' to it gangsta rap made
    me do it

ICE CUBE
(from "Gangsta Rap Made Me Do It"
on his *Raw Footage* album)

He has told you, O man, what is good;
    And what does the LORD require of you
but to do justice, and to love kindness,
    and to walk humbly with your God?

MICAH 6:8

4

GANGSTA RAP MADE ME DO IT: WHAT'S REALLY GOIN' ON?

Ralph C. Watkins

It is hard to listen to rap music. I don't know about you, but for me it is sometimes difficult to have an appreciation for hip-hop culture. There is a lot about hip-hop that makes me cringe and at times scream. While this is the case, I am still compelled to listen. I am called to lean in and hear what's going on in the lives of the hip-hop generation. Those things that repel me are worthy of criticism. The American values of lust, misogyny, sexism, greed, materialism, hypersexuality, and violence that I hear in rap music and commercialized hip-hop culture have to be addressed. They make me sick to my stomach. There is room for criticism of rap music and commercialized hip-hop culture. In this chapter I will try to bring balance to the conversation. While the critics of hip-hop are many, and with a valid argument, those who have leaned in to listen with an empathetic ear tend to be in the minority, especially when it comes to the church. I am not defending hip-hop, but I am asking that we listen a little more carefully. I am appealing to the church to be a loving community that hears the pain and heals the wounds. I am arguing that the problems our young adults and youths are facing are bigger than hip-hop, and we can't place all the blame on hip-hop, though hip-hop does have to bear some degree of the blame. A deeper socio-demographic-theological analysis is needed if the church is to respond effectively to the hip-hop generation and heal the wounds of despair and alienation that exist between the hip-hop generation and their elders.

On Ice Cube's *Raw Footage* CD, in his song "Gangsta Rap Made Me Do It" he rings out in each chorus, "gangsta rap made me do it."[1] The chorus at the beginning of this chapter is the second of the three different choruses in the song that identify the things gangsta rap is blamed for. In each chorus what gangsta rap is blamed for is changed and becomes ever more outrageous. In the third chorus Ice Cube says, "If I f_ _ _ up the planet ain't nothin' to it gangsta rap made me do it." What Ice Cube is exposing is how gangsta rap is blamed for the ills of society. Don't worry about what you do, whether you are a rapper, a kid from the hood, a preacher, or even a white radio talk show host, "If I call you a nappy headed ho ain't nothin' to it gangsta rap made [Don Imus] me do it." Ice Cube is pointing out that human behavior is much more complex than being the result of a single variable. The struggles that African-American youths and young adults are facing can't be blamed on hip-hop. This is the point Ice Cube is trying to make. When you put Ice Cube in dialogue with Bill Cosby and Alvin Poussaint, it should at least make us think. Ice Cube is chosen as a dialogical partner because he is one of the founders of what Cosby and Poussaint point to in hip-hop culture as the culprit, gangsta rap. So what is the historical foundation of gangsta rap?

In 1988 NWA dropped the classic album *Straight Outta Compton*, and it is really at this point in hip-hop history that the West Coast got national attention from the hip-hop community. Jerry Heller and Eric Eazy E were the masterminds behind the exposure that the group received. But more than savvy marketing and a shocking name was the story that *Straight Outta Compton* told. It told a story of what the group called "street knowledge." These men, then young brothers, were coming, as they said on the opening track, "Straight Outta Compton." The story opens with them announcing who they were and where they were coming from, "Straight outta Compton mother f_ _ _ _ _ named Ice Cube from the

---

[1] Ice Cube, *Raw Footage*, Lench Mob Records, 2008.

gang called Niggaz With Attitudes." They were boyz from the hood who had something to say, and they were going to say it with an attitude. The next logical question is, why did they have an attitude? The reason they had an attitude was because they had been abused by the police. Not only them, but they make it clear in the story that the police are a part of the larger systemic problem of racism and classism. If the listener missed this in the opening song/story, it came through loud and clear in the next cut, "F_ _ _ tha Police." NWA saw themselves as a different kind of a gang, but they were a gang.

NWA, the fathers of gangsta rap, were a gang that was designated to be the griots or storytellers of the pain that their brothas and sistas in the hood on the West Coast were going through. Eithne Quinn's book *Nuthin' but a "G" Thang: The Culture and Commerce of Gangsta Rap* tells how this revolutionary story of exposing pain became a product for sale to the highest bidder. While Quinn's assessment and link with gangsta rap and commercialization singles out what happened with West Coast hip-hop culture, the story isn't unpredictable. Hip-hop culture was being bottled and sold in the early 1990s. Jerry Heller and others like him were now on board, and the days of the mid-1970s (the birth of hip-hop culture, which would later be exploited by the hip-hop industry) would never be again. The story of the West is chronicled not only in Eithne Quinn's book but also in William Shaw's *Westside: The Coast-to-Coast Explosion of Hip-hop*. We can also read a complementary commentary to the work of Eithne Quinn in Ronin Ro's book *Gangsta: Merchandising the Rhymes of Violence*. Finally there is Joel McIver's book *Ice Cube Attitude*. Much of the West Coast history is found in the work of Too Short, Ice T, NWA, Dr. Dre, Snoop Dogg, The Dogg Pound, Daz and Kurupt, and of course Ice Cube, especially after he left NWA. The work of the artist in hip-hop culture tells more about the culture than do the books that are published on the topic. Those of us who write about the culture are trying to interpret for our readers, but I want to encourage readers to become listeners, watchers, and participants of hip-hop culture.

It is important to go back to the original sources. If one wants to learn the story of West Coast hip-hop culture, one is encouraged to listen to that story straight from those who tell the story in time and rhyme.

When you go back and listen to the dialogical partner in this chapter, Ice Cube (O'Shea Jackson), the son of a two-parent home, you hear a young man who was all about reporting what he saw in the hood and not promoting violence. In many ways Ice Cube is a participant-observer, in the traditional sociological sense, when it comes to his reporting on the violence, poverty, and struggle of the inner-city poor in Los Angeles. The concern I have with some critics of hip-hop is that in most cases their critique, which tends to be shallow and surface, proves that they haven't listened intently to hip-hop culture nor engaged the complex stories in rap lyrics. It was in high school that Ice Cube, the son of parents who worked at UCLA (his mother was an active member at Bethel African Methodist Episcopal Church in Los Angeles), began to write his rhymes that were telling the story of his times. Ice Cube was the first member of NWA. When NWA hit the rap scene on the West Coast, they were compared to Public Enemy of the East Coast. These were conscious rap groups that were raising issues and fighting against the system. Ice Cube's eventually leaving the NWA and striking out on his own was his personal stand against what he saw as the hip-hop industry's pimping and abuse of hip-hop culture.

Ice Cube is the father of gangsta rap, and he has a right to that legacy. On his *Laugh Now, Cry Later* CD on the cut "Child Support," Ice Cube critiques the direction of some rap artists who claim to be heirs of the gangsta rap subgenre.[2] As the father of gangsta rap, Ice Cube stands as a senior critic who in his early forties is saying that some of the music is not reflective of a true West Coast gangsta. A true West Coast gangsta like Ice Cube is one who is the hood's CNN. They aren't promoting violence; they are critiquing the social conditions that create, sustain, and maintain conditions for the violence they see in the hood. Ice Cube's body of work from

---

[2] Ice Cube, *Laugh Now, Cry Later*, Lench Mob Records, 2006.

1988 to the present, as the father of gangsta rap, has been both socially conscious and critical of the oppressive forces that have produced what we see in the inner cities of America. On his *Laugh Now, Cry Later* CD cut, "Why We Thugs" he is clear that the conditions of poverty in inner cities are not the result of gangsta rap.[3] Ice Cube asserts that forces outside of the hood send in guns and drugs, two keys as to why what happens happens in the hood. Ice Cube talks about the deplorable working conditions and the lack of jobs that create a crime frenzy in the hood, the decaying social networks, the dilapidated civic organizations—and you want to blame gangsta rap? Ice Cube recognizes the limitations of the self-help theory. Noted sociologist William J. Wilson put it this way:

For the first time in the twentieth century most adults in many inner city ghetto neighborhoods are not working in a typical week. The disappearance of work has adversely affected not only individuals, families, and neighborhoods, but the social life of the city at large as well. . . . A neighborhood in which people are poor but employed is different from a neighborhood in which people are poor and jobless. Many of today's problems in the inner-city ghetto neighborhoods—crime, family dissolution, welfare, low levels of social organization, and so on—are fundamentally a consequence of the disappearance of work.[4]

What Wilson and Ice Cube are saying is that if you want to understand what is happening in the hood, one has to point the finger at an infrastructure that has been destroyed over the last forty years.

What Wilson and Ice Cube are eluding to in their work is that the issue isn't gangsta rap or the decay of values in the communities of poor African-Americans but larger systemic issues. In fairness to Poussaint and Cosby, they point to these forces but fail to take into account just how powerful they are in the lives of those who are

[3]Ibid.
[4]William J. Wilson, *When Work Disappears: The World of the New Urban Poor* (New York: Vintage Books, 1996), xiiii.

trying to make it in the hood. Cosby and Poussaint say, "Gangster rap . . . promotes the moral breakdown of the family. It deliberately influences women to become pregnant before they have finished their education and influences men to shuck their responsibility when this happens."[5] Cosby and Poussaint go on to use a scene from a fictional movie, 8 Mile, as an example to amplify their point. "In the climactic scene in the film 8 Mile, Eminem disses Papa Doc, his black opponent in a freestyle rap showdown, for being named 'Clarence' and having 'two parents.' The wound is lethal. Eminem prevails. In the world of hip-hop, to be educated as Papa Doc was, and to live in the suburb with both parents, is to be less 'black' than even a white guy."[6] But Cosby and Poussaint miss the point of the scene. Eminem isn't dissing Clarence because of social status and family lifestyle. The dis is based on Clarence's trying to pretend those things aren't true of him. The name Papa Doc and pretending to be hard and from the hood is what exposes Clarence. Clarence was rapping a lie; hip-hop calls for authenticity. If you are going to talk about the hood and represent the hood, then you have to really be from the hood. 50 Cent really did get shot. Jay-Z, Biggie, and Tupac did have struggles growing up. DMX really did do time. Eminem was poor. Gangsta rap isn't promoting; rather real gangsta rap is about reporting.

William J. Wilson says, "Our research reveals that the beliefs of inner-city residents bear little resemblance to the blanket media reports asserting that values have plummeted in impoverished neighborhoods or that people in the inner city have an entirely different value system. What is so striking is that despite the overwhelming joblessness and poverty, black residents in inner-city ghetto neighborhoods actually verbally endorse, rather than undermine, the basic American values concerning individual initiative."[7] Values have not plummeted; inner-city African-Americans embrace mainstream values. They want the good job, house, white picket

---

[5]Bill Cosby and Alvin F. Poussaint, *Come On People: On the Path from Victims to Victors* (Nashville: Thomas Nelson, 2007), 143.
[6]Ibid.
[7]Wilson, *When Work Disappears*, 179.

fence, dog, minivan, and 2.5 kids. The reality is that the structural forces are so strong that they impede inner-city African-Americans' ability to fulfill the American dream. Gangsta rap isn't stopping them or even encouraging them not to dream. When you listen to hip-hop, it is thoroughly American. Hip-hop is capitalism at its best. Hip-hop's story is, a broke kid from the ghetto works hard, makes beats, writes rhymes, gets signed by a major label, and makes it good. Hip-hop is the Horatio Alger myth on steroids. Hip-hop artists don't dis American values; just like poor inner-city African-Americans, they are trying to live the American dream while living in an American nightmare.

The reality is that when young African-Americans go looking for jobs, they find that the jobs simply aren't there. The key argument in William J. Wilson's book *When Work Disappears: The World of the New Urban Poor*, which is supported with hard research, is simply what the title says: work has disappeared. The employment base for the inner-city poor isn't there. There aren't enough jobs to support them. When inner-city African-Americans compete for the few jobs that do exist, they face overwhelming odds as they confront what is gently referred to by Wilson as "selective recruitment." African-Americans are denied an opportunity to work. "Selective recruitment practices do represent what economists call statistical discrimination: employers make assumptions about inner-city black workers in general and reach decisions based on those assumptions before they have had a chance to review systematically the qualifications of an individual applicant. The net effect is that many black inner-city applicants are never given the chance to prove their qualifications on an individual level because they are systematically screened out by the selective recruitment process."[8] In the end we have two key variables at work—lack of jobs and then racial/class discrimination when inner-city African-Americans apply for jobs. These two variables have nothing to do with gangsta rap. At the foundation of the problems in the hood is the systemic forces that have worked

[8]Ibid., 137.

against African-American working class progress. The conversation of Cosby and Poussaint put in a book is evidence for a social constructed reality that is not based on research. As one reads the unbalanced critique of hip-hop and the blame game that Cosby, Poussaint, and their callouts suggest, one has to stop and reflect on the question, can their assertions be supported by empirical data? What the empirical data tells us is that in the final analysis gangsta rap and hip-hop culture have had little to do with creating the world of the inner-city poor.

This generation of inner-city poor African-Americans are trying to make it in an economy that has transitioned from an industrial economy to a service economy. They are going to public schools that are overcrowded, underfunded, and understaffed. As Joan Morgan says of the hip-hop generation, "We are the first generation to grow up with all the benefits of Civil Rights (i.e., Affirmative Action, government-subsidized educational and social programs) and the first to lose them. The first to have the devastation of AIDS, crack, and black-on-black violence makes it feel like a blessing to reach twenty-five."[9] The odds are stacked against them; but gangsta rap didn't create these conditions. The world in which inner-city African-Americans live isn't that enclave of class diversity that my generation was raised in; these residents are socially isolated and socially dislocated. They live in communities that are filled with poor, unemployed neighbors who can't help them get a job. As a result they are not connected to the workforce, as Wacquant and Wilson suggest:

> The poor are presented as a mere aggregation of personal cases, each with its own logic and self-contained causes. Severed from the struggles and structural changes in the society, economy, and polity that in fact determine them, inner-city dislocations are then portrayed as a self-imposed, self-sustaining phenomenon . . . the urban black poor today differ both from their counterparts of earlier years and from the white poor in that they are becoming

---

[9]Joan Morgan, *When Chickenheads Come Home to Roost . . . My Life as a Hip-Hop Feminist* (New York: Simon & Schuster, 1999), 61.

increasingly concentrated in dilapidated territorial enclaves that
epitomize acute social and economic marginalization. . . . The
economic and social buffer provided by a stable black working
class and a visible, if small, black middle class that cushioned the
impact of downsizing in the economy and tied ghetto residents to
the world of work has all but disappeared. Moreover, the social
networks of parents, friends, and associates, as well as the nexus
of local institutions, have seen their resources for economic stability progressively depleted. In sum, today's ghetto residents face a
closed opportunity structure.[10]

A closed opportunity structure. This is the reality. It isn't
gangsta rap that has closed the door on opportunity for inner-city
African-Americans. In the words of Biggie, "Things done changed."
If the church is going to respond prophetically to this crisis, it must
realize that *things done changed* and the church has to engage the
powers that be to kick open the doors of opportunity.

THINGS DONE CHANGED: A CALL FOR A PROPHETIC ENCOUNTER

He has told you, O man, what is good;
    and what does the LORD require of you
but to do justice, and to love kindness,
    and to walk humbly with your God? (Micah 6:8)

Gangster rap makes our young people tough, but not so tough
that they can walk through prison walls. It can jazz them about
sex, but it can't begin to make them good fathers. No matter how
often or how publicly they grab their crotches, crotch-grabbing
isn't even going to get them a bus ride downtown.[11]

The ghetto is a nigga trap, take the cheese
Soon as you do it here come the police
Invented and designed fo' us to fail
Where you gon' end up, dead or in jail

[10]Loïc J. D. Wacquant and William Julius Wilson, "The Cost of Racial and Class Exclusion in
the Inner City," *The Ghetto Underclass: Social Science Perspectives*, ed. William Julius Wilson
(Newbury Park, CA: SAGE Publications, 1993), 25–26.
[11]Cosby and Poussaint, *Come On People*, 13.

Concrete slave ships, never move
Where niggaz like us get used like a mule
Don't let em catch you, arrest you
Strip and undress you, throw you in a cesspool

You wanna know the crime of the century
A ghetto elementary, a mental penitentiary
Black man, you never been friend of me
Boy you kin to me, why we enemies?
The ghetto is a trap[12]

When you actually consider the father of gangsta rap, Ice Cube, carefully, what you see is not the monolith that some critics want to present. Instead you hear a social critic engaging the social conditions of the hood and speaking prophetically. In the quote above you hear Ice Cube being tough, but he isn't promoting black on black violence, he isn't promoting toughness. Ice Cube says, "Boy you kin to me, why we enemies?" He is saying we should not be shooting each other. He is asking young brothers and sisters to sit back and reflect. We are not meant to be enemies. He is pointing out how "the ghetto" is a "trap" that has been socially constructed by an economic system that is designed to profit from the pain of the poor. The trap is set to lead young African-Americans into a life of crime and violence. A chess game of crime and violence is set in the trap, and the trapdoor is the prison door that slams shut. Ice Cube isn't leading kids to walk through that door; he is trying to help them see how they are being set up to be lifelong slaves in a prison industry. A school system that ill equips kids to succeed ensures that prison and the inner city become nothing less than concrete slave ships. Ice Cube is prophetically critiquing what he calls a new form of slavery. The socio-critical-prophetic voice of hip-hop needs to be heard here. If we listen to Ice Cube, we will hear him say this is part of the problem. As Dyson puts it, ". . . the arguments of many of hip hop's critics demand little engagement with hip hop. Their

---

[12]Ice Cube, "The Nigga Trap," *Laugh Now, Cry Later.*

views don't require much beyond attending to the surface symptoms of a culture that offers far more depth and color when it is taken seriously and criticized thoughtfully. . . . Such critics seem afraid of the intellectual credibility or complex truths they might find were they to surrender their sideline seat and take an analytical plunge into the culture on which they comment."[13] I will admit there are problems with hip-hop and some manifestations of gangsta rap, but if the church doesn't take the art form seriously by embracing it in a conversation, the church may miss the complexities, cries, and truths that are coming out of hip-hop. As Dyson suggests, there is room for critique, but there is also room for affirmation and an ear for the prophetic pronouncements that come out of hip-hop.

Marvin McMickle in his book *Where Have All the Prophets Gone?* calls the church to the task of being prophetic. In order for the church to return to this sacred practice, what we hear from the pulpit has to change. This is a call for prophetic preaching. McMickle says, "Prophetic preaching points out the false gods of comfort. Further, it points out a lack of concern and acquiescence in the face of evil that can so easily replace the true God of scripture who calls true believers to the active pursuit of justice and righteousness for every member of society. Prophetic preaching also never allows the community of faith to believe that participation in the rituals of religious life can ever be an adequate substitute for that form of ministry that is designed to uplift the 'least of these' in our world."[14] To act prophetically means that the church must engage the world. The church must hear the cry of hip-hop and speak back prophetically. The church must be a theological partner in the dialogue with artists like Ice Cube. While Ice Cube has the social critique down, and he even calls the church to task, the church has to offer a theological analysis of what is going on in the hood.

The church's critique and prophetic voice has to be rooted in the tradition of Amos, Jeremiah, and Micah. The theological and

---

[13]Michael Eric Dyson, *Know What I Mean? Reflections on Hip Hop* (New York: Basic Civitas Books, 2007), xxi.
[14]Marvin McMickle, *Where Have All the Prophets Gone? Reclaiming Prophetic Preaching in America* (Cleveland: The Pilgrim Press, 2006), 2.

biblical engagement of the church must be rooted in the witness of Jesus who shouts in Luke 4:18 that He came "to proclaim liberty to the captives" and then in Matthew 25:31–46, "Truly, I say to you, as you did it to one of the least of these my brothers, you did it to me." Part of the theological response is a call to action—to understand how the social structures of a stratified society that keeps the poor poor and makes the rich wealthier needs to be critiqued based on the witness of Jesus who came to set the captives free. As McMickle says, "The prophets preached truth to power, attacking the monarchs and the ruling elite."[15] While Ice Cube calls the powers that be out and says they are creating stationary slave ships, the church has been silent. Ice Cube is pointing to the fact that the absence of prophetic preaching implicates the church in the creation of the current conditions against which inner-city African-Americans are struggling to survive. Ice Cube says, on the cut "Thank God" on his *Raw Footage* CD:

I do gangsta rap
They wanna blame world problems on gangsta rap
It's our fault, cause motherf_ _ _ _ _ _ is dying in Iraq
It's our fault, cause motherf_ _ _ _ _ _ is starving in Africa
It's gangsta rap's fault that people are poor
Can't get enough to f_ _ _ _ _ eat or live their life
That's rap music fault
It's rap music fault, that we got all this godd_ _ _ laws
and restriction and s_ _ _ we can't do
They blame it all on us
I'm blamin' them for gangsta rap,
because if they didn't create this kind of condition
I wouldn't have s_ _ _ to rap about
You know what I mean?[16]

Do we know what he means? He is pointing the finger back at the church. Is Ice Cube saying we are blaming gangsta rap for creating the conditions that he raps about? No! Ice Cube is saying that

---
[15]Ibid, 3.
[16]Ice Cube, "Thank God," *Raw Footage.*

the prophetic call reverses the blame game and realizes that what Jesus said in Matthew 7:1–5 about pointing fingers and judging others is true. The church has to deal with its plank. What can't the church see? Can the church see what has caused and continues to cause the conditions under which poor inner-city African-Americans are laboring? If the church listened to hip-hop as a weeping prophet, how would that change its take on gangsta rap?

Part of the active socio-theological response of the church has to be the practice of sacred listening. I am convinced that hip-hop has not been heard by the church. The cry, the pain, the sense of abandonment by elders, a lack of appreciation for the art of hip-hop has not been heard. The hip-hop generation is in pain. Joan Morgan, the hip-hop feminist, tells us why she listens and why we should listen. Morgan says, "My decision to expose myself to the sexism of Dr. Dre, Ice Cube, Snoop Dogg, or the Notorious B.I.G. is really my plea to my brothers to tell me who they are. As a black woman and a feminist I listen to the music with a willingness to see past the machismo in order to be clear about what I am really dealing with. . . . I believe hip-hop can help us win. Let's start by recognizing that its illuminating, informative narration and its incredible ability to articulate our collective pain is an invaluable tool when examining gender relations. The information we amass can help create a redemptive, healing space for brothers and sistas."[17] When we listen with ears of love, we hear the hurt, we hear the pain. While hip-hop artists shout more loudly and more angrily, we have to ask whether this is because they feel like they haven't been heard. Why does Ice Cube in his forties run around defending his art form that he has been developing for over twenty years? Ice Cube, a businessman, father, husband, movie star, and gangsta rapper/prophet, still has to scream because the elders refuse to listen. The interesting thing about Jesus was, he always had time to listen. Jesus heard the cries for help. Jesus had time to stop and heal, to resurrect and give hope.

A prophetic response via preaching and social action from the

---

[17]Joan Morgan, *When Chickenheads Come Home to Roost*, 80.

church should not simply condemn the abuses of capitalism. Rather as McMickle says, "The great need that faces preaching today and that is badly needed by the people who hear that preaching is the reclaiming of this tension between action and accountability, between distributive and redistributive justice, between obeying God's command to do the work of justice and facing God's judgment and wrath when we fail or refuse to do so."[18] The church must embrace this tension of action and accountability as it does the work of justice. What does this mean? It means the church doesn't have to excuse hip-hop, but it must lovingly approach hip-hop with informed engagement that is contextualized in present social realities of oppression. The church must look inwardly and critique itself or at least listen to the critique that the hip-hop generation has by and large lodged at the church. The silence of the church's prophetic voice and engagement with youths and young adult culture has made the church irrelevant in the lives of most young, inner-city African-Americans.

It was in the 1990s that C. Eric Lincoln cried out about the pending irrelevance of the African-American church. Did the church hear him? C. Eric Lincoln and Lawrence Mamiya said, "A major challenge to the Black Church concerns a growing sector of unchurched black youth, largely teenage and young adult black males from the underclass."[19] This growing sector of unchurched black youth and young adults still remains unchurched and untouched. Where do they lodge their cry? Who comes to their aid? Who walks with them? Who talks with them? Who develops them? Do they feel heard in hip-hop? Do they feel loved by hip-hop? Has hip-hop become their pastor?

PRAYING FOR OUR CHILDREN AND YOUNG ADULTS

What I suggest in the end is that churches start by listening to hip-hop. There are the radio cuts, or what we call club bangers, that

---

[18]McMickle, *Where Have All the Prophets Gone?*, 46.
[19]C. Eric Lincoln and Lawrence H. Mamiya, *The Black Church in African American Experience* (Durham and London: Duke University Press, 1990), 322.

will repel most church folk right away, because in most cases they represent the worst of hip-hop culture that has been abused by the hip-hop industry. Therefore let me suggest a first-stage listening list or playlist to begin to engage the conversation and practice of sacred listening. I would suggest the following cuts:

- Mack 10—"The Testimony" on his *Hustla's Handbook* CD
- Ice Cube—"Why We Thugs" on his *Laugh Now, Cry Later* CD
- Ice Cube—"Gangsta Rap Made Me Do It" on his *Raw Footage* CD
- The Game—"My Life" on his *LAX Files* CD
- T.I.—"Prayin for Help" on his *Urban Legend* CD
- Lil Wayne—"Tie My Hands" on his *Tha Carter III* CD
- Faboloos—"Stay" on his *Loso's Way* CD
- Pharrel—"Our Father" on his *In My Mind* CD
- Kanye West—"Pinocchio Story" on his *808s Heartbreak* CD
- Jay-Z—"Lost One" on his *Kingdom Come* CD
- Talib Kweli—"Black Girl Pain" on his *The Beautiful Struggle* CD

These songs will give the church an initial window into the heart of hip-hop. The songs can be purchased individually via a digital store like iTunes, or CDs can be purchased via any record store. If this is believers' first engagement with hip-hop I would suggest they buy edited versions of the music (hip-hop records have both edited and unedited versions). The unedited versions include cursing, and some church members might not want to hear the profanity.

Are we prepared to listen and respect each other? If not, how do we get to that point? I want to suggest that elder believers must provide the leadership God has called them to provide. We are the ones who need to step forward and call our people into the kitchen as we prepare a meal and initiate discussion. We can take the first step by setting the table, then ask our younger sisters and brothers to begin the dialogue. That's right, we ask them to start us off. We should have begun the listening process prior to dinner. We should watch their culture as it is portrayed in accessible formats. This means we can watch some videos, listen to the radio, or better yet make our way to the local book and record store and carefully select the voices we choose to hear. We may want to select those more conscious voices that don't get radio airtime. My only caution would be that we don't ignore the more commercial aspects of hip-hop because it has a greater hold on our youth and young adults. We may want to simply begin by having mini-conversations in many places with those who look like us but are much younger than us. We may call nephews or nieces and listen while they talk. We have to make room for them to be honest about us, the church, and our faith tradition. This conversation must be rooted in love. We have to suspend our desire to defend our ways and be willing to engage in give-and-take conversation that moves us closer together in spite of our generational divides.

Through the power of language we tell the story in our own words. Ngugi wa Thiong'o tells us that language carries culture.[20] We must speak in our language. We must use the rhythm, style, tone, and lyricism of our language to tell the story. This means we must make room for a time to tell our stories. We must re-create the kitchens and the sitting rooms of our culture. The village cannot be sustained without intentional times of sharing. We must listen to some of hip-hop's most outspoken leaders. When we listen and talk to them, we will hear the ancestors leading us back while pointing us forward. We have to take the walks in the park to which Jill Scott has called us. We have to look for Zion with Lauryn Hill. We have to come and hear the political rhetoric of Mos Def and Dead Prez as they critique the very system or industry that produces the worst and best of hip-hop. We have to answer the call to discipleship as ushered by Nas. We even have to go to Chicago and testify with Common and Kanye West as they raise the right questions in their complex works. There is a word in hip-hop, and there is a word on the streets, in the academy, and in the church. These worlds that are built on the Word must be brought

---

[20]Ngugi wa Thiong'o, *Decolonising the Mind: The Politics of Language in African Literature* (London: J. Currey/Portsmouth, N.H.: Heinemann, 1986).

into a concerted family conversation about who we've been, who we are, and who shall we become.

We have to go back to the basics. The church has to reach out and reach up. God is love, and God is calling the church to love the hip-hop generation. As elders we have the responsibility to call the children in the house for a conversation. I remember growing up in the South and my mother calling me into the house when the streetlights came on. I hated that call, and I loved that call. I never wanted to stop playing, but there was no more secure place than home at my mother's dinner table. The love and support I found in our home is what propelled me to get up the next day and do it all again. It is time for us to call hip-hop to church and to say, "We love you, and we are glad you are at the table. Now let's talk." In the end this is about discipleship and spiritual maturity. How can the church help our young people see where hip-hop is good and where it has gone wrong as it has emulated the larger popular culture? In discipleship we don't excuse our young people but rather lovingly develop them. I am reminded of Proverbs 22:6:

> Train up a child in the way he [she] should go; even when he [she] is old he [she] will not depart from it.

I ask the question, have we trained the children? If the promise implied in the text is true, then we have to ask, why are so many departing? Some may say I am just proof-texting. Maybe, but the question still remains, have we trained them? When I visit churches with empty Sunday school rooms, micro-Bible studies, and part-time youth ministries I wonder, when did this happen? This is not the church I was raised in with full Sunday schools and well-attended Bible studies. On one hand we have to hold hip-hop accountable for its wrongs, and on the other hand we have to assume our responsibility as the church to reach the young and teach them the Scriptures and what it means to live according to the Word of God. I was taught. I was raised by my nuclear family and by a little church, St. James African Methodist Episcopal Church in Eatonville, Florida, which taught me to love God, respect women, and not be trapped by the ways of the world. As I have gotten old, I haven't departed from what they taught me. Let us be about our Father's business and train our children in the gospel.

5

BLACK MEN AND MASCULINITY

Eric M. Mason

Recently much discussion has occurred attempting to assess the issues that blacks face in America and the problems faced in the uniqueness of our journey. Many have highlighted important issues, but the solutions are too multifaceted, comprehensive, and systemic to make simplistic applications. Moreover, all of these must flow from the transforming power of the gospel of Jesus Christ (Romans 1:16).

UNFAIR COMPARISONS

As I heard one man give a historical layout of masculinity, it was obvious that his vision was drawn from the perspective of white men in America. It is impossible to talk about manhood in the experience of black men without a basic overview of black history. It has been said that history is the road map for what to do and what not to do. I have heard much about manhood in my life as a Christian man, but most of it has come from white Christendom. Sometimes I hear great information but feel unclear about the idea's historical background.

On one occasion I was going through some manhood material contextualized for suburban, white, middle- or upper-class men. The information and curriculum was excellent, but one section of the material disturbed me. The section was entitled "The Historical Roots to Our Present Crisis in Masculinity."[1] The author spoke of

---

[1]Robert Lewis, *The Quest for Authentic Manhood*, DVD (Fellowship Bible Church, Little Rock, Arkansas, 2004).

the sociological place of manhood during the Industrial Revolution (the first occurring in the eighteenth century and the second during the nineteenth century) and during World War II (1939–1945).

This same time period, viewed from an African-American perspective, would consist of drastically different key events and figures, such as slavery, Jim Crow, the Civil Rights Movement, the Black Power/Black Bourgeoisie era, the Soul Baby Era, the hip-hop generation, and the Eclectic era. What has driven black history in America is the fight for freedom. For many it is the fight to experience what has almost always been available to whites. Blacks and whites are on two completely different sociological and economic planes. The fight for blacks has been off balance because our expectations have been shaped by the experiences of white Americans. Because of this, we have settled for both an American experience viewed through the eyes of whites and a Christian experience that reflects that of our white brethren. Because of all this, we must show that the social issues each race must deal with are extremely different, although all are a result of the fall. We must remember that Jesus, not another man, is the one who gives us our image of the ideal man; He embodied true humanity. With this in mind, we must be willing to transport our vision of christology across the bounds of various social, cultural, and ethnic barriers. We will discuss this in more detail later.

During slavery, black men were emasculated by not being allowed to marry, either at all or only to women on the same plantation,[2] being forced to watch black women become the unwed playthings of white slave owners, etc. We could go on until the break of dawn.

In the post-slavery Jim Crow South, blacks were free from slavery, but racism and repression were as strong as ever. The doctrine of "separate but equal" was intended to maintain equality between the races while preventing the civil strife that would supposedly result from mixing the two races. However, in reality this principle became another means of repressing blacks. Blacks and whites were

---

[2]John Hope Franklin and Alfred A. Moss Jr., *From Slavery to Freedom: A History of African Americans*, eighth edition (Boston: McGraw-Hill, 2000), 127–128.

certainly kept separate, but the opportunities afforded each race were hardly equal.

The civil rights era is known to many blacks as the golden years. Black leaders developed a vision for practical equality that inspired many. But this vision was still void of an image of masculinity. Masculinity to the African-American was still viewed in terms of the social displays of freedom that were portrayed in (white) majority culture. Even the images and comprehensive character of Jesus were portrayed without a proper view of biblical masculinity.

The black power side of the post–civil rights generation sought to create a new path and image, forged by blacks, for blacks in America. "The Movement" was committed to a rigorous affirmation of blackness, racial pride, and an insistence on the economic and political liberation of black people, independent of whites.[3] During this period, masculinity was expressed through art, fashion, black intellectualism, and historical identification with African roots. Blacks became extremely proud of their heritage, but something was still missing, as comparisons to white America were still the measuring rod for black progress.

The black bourgeoisie were a different breed of blacks who were socialized during and after the Civil Rights Movement. They were the first to reap the rewards of that movement. Many black nationalists viewed them as sellouts. E. Franklin Frazier states:

> In attempting to escape identification with the black masses, they have developed a self-hatred that reveals itself in their depreciation of the physical and social characteristics of Negroes. Likewise, their feelings of inferiority and insecurity are revealed in their pathological struggle for status within the isolated Negro world and craving recognition in the white world.[4]

As harsh as this analysis is, it serves as an apt summary for

[3]Jeffrey Ogbonna Green Obgar, *Black Power: Radical Politics and African American Identity* (Baltimore: John Hopkins University Press, 2004), 37.
[4]E. Franklin Frazier, *Black Bourgeoisie: The Book That Brought the Shock of Self-Revelation to Middle-Class Blacks in America* (New York: Free Press Paperbacks, 1997), 213.

the previous points. Masculinity during this era was still being defined according to the definition proposed by white America. Art attempted to paint a multifaceted image of black manhood during the 1970s, even with blaxploitation movies. "Masculinity" was all over the place. *Shaft*, *The Jeffersons*, and *Good Times* were some of the most prevalent models of that period. Our current society still bears the effects of these images. In addition, the black preacher and the church were seen as the worse image of manhood in America. These points are not intended to place blame on white America for black issues but rather to partially explain why things are the way they are today.

THE HIP-HOP/SOUL ERA

The Hip-Hop/Soul Era is becoming more of an eclectic movement in our contemporary culture. However, hip-hop has been one of the most profound global influences on multiple cultures since the rise of rock. Its influence has spread to every continent except Antarctica, and it continues to expand and diversify its subgenres. As it relates to masculinity, hip-hop culture has been critiqued and criticized on many occasions. Whether it is gangster rap, pimpology, extravagance unleashed, womanizing, Islamic underpinnings, or whatever, hip-hop has had its share of troubles when it comes to scrutiny of its influence on both men and women. Along with all of its components that people would have trouble with, hip-hop presents a skewed image of black men.

Whether we admit it or not, art has had an undeniable influence on culture's perception of manhood. Though many are able to identify with the indigenous connectivity of hip-hop culture, many of its components are irredeemable. Hip-hop has made both positive and negative contributions to the masculinity of black men. One negative effect is the insatiable need to amass wealth, glorified in much of hip-hop. As spoken by the West Coast poet Warren G:

I want it all; money, fast cars
Diamond rings, gold chains and champagne . . .

I want it all; houses, expenses
My own business, a truck, hmm, and a couple o' Benz's
I want it all; brand new socks and drawls
And I'm ballin everytime I stop and talk to y'all
I want it all, all, all, all
I want it all, all, all, all, all.[5]

THE ECLECTIC ERA

The Eclectic Era has had a great impact on culture's view of masculinity. In what many consider an era in which white racial and ethnic issues are less discernible or less understood by the those under age forty, a fusion of the arts and gender specificity has become normal. This era is filled with positives but also has many negative repercussions in relation to masculinity. What manhood looks like is determined by the roles one accepts in society, one's attitude toward other people, and even the clothing one wears.

Jay-Z released an album on September 11, 2009 called *The Blueprint 3*. He has proven to not only be a trendsetter artistically but also in people's understanding of manhood and maturity. On the day of the album's release, he had a live concert on the Fuse website. In an interview before the concert, he stated his desire to transform the art of hip-hop, especially the content that artists are coming out with. One of the most profound statements that he made was on race. Jay stated that because of the global-local ("glocal") connection of the arts and technology, black and white issues have taken a backseat to issues affecting the global multi-ethnic community. His point was that people are gathering around what connects, rather than divides, them.

His track "Death of Auto-Tune" is a call to musical authenticity and the execution of true talent, but the call is masculine in tone. Jay-Z speaks to rappers not only about the heart and soul of hip-hop but also about the elements missing from its culture of masculinity.

For black men who had not had any cultural identity, hip-hop provided a vision. When we saw the Motown artists—as much as

---

[5]Warren G, "I Want It All," *I Want It All*, Restless Records, 1999.

we enjoyed their music—before the 1970s, we weren't dreaming the way they were. During the crack era and the creation of turbulent inner cities, we were caught between a rock and a hard place. In light of this, hip-hop was indigenous, and it gave vision (through the creation of music videos, BET, and later MTV) of what an external manhood could look like. Out of all the other parts of history, hip-hop gave us the most vivid images of manhood—images of violence and rage providing (illegitimately and without redemptive value) lust, love, and, most importantly, freedom.

CONTEMPORARY SIGNIFICANCE

Today images of masculinity appear to be a casualty of history. Many have attempted to defuse this claim, but everything unredeemed is a casualty of the fall, whether it be human nature or the world in which we live. Because of this, we hear about statistics that reflect some type of connection.

Cosby and Poussaint, in their book *Come On People*, reveal some startling statistics.

In the past several decades, the suicide rate among young black men has increased 100 percent. In some cities black males have high school dropout rates of more than 50 percent. Young black men are twice as likely to be unemployed as white, Hispanic, and Asian men. Although black people make up just 12 percent of the general population, they make up nearly 44 percent of the prison population (some statistics state 75 percent of the prison population is African-American). These are just some of the figures indicating that something is severely wrong with many young black men's understanding of masculinity. The solution to this problem can only be achieved through a biblical understanding of masculinity.

"Yo Brutha, where you at?" This is the most riveting question in the Bible. As a matter of fact, this was the first recorded question asked by God in the Scriptures: "But the LORD God called to the man and said to him, 'Where are you?'" (Genesis 3:9). Yahweh's asking this question is one of the most powerful scenes in the Bible.

After Adam and Eve disobey God, the Missionary God goes after them and calls out to them. The omnipotent, omniscient, and omnipresent God calls out to the man, making it clear that God uniquely holds the man as spokesperson for both himself and Eve. Infinite principles can be gleaned from this question, but we will limit our discussion to only three.

God Was Not Lost—The Man Was

God went looking for the man. He is still doing so, but He is also forging biblical men after the image of Christ (Romans 8:29; Colossians 1:15). God is not only looking for men but is re-creating them as well (John 3:5). Through Jesus Christ, God is reconciling all things to Himself (Colossians 1:20). Everything redeemable that lost its place because of the fall, God is bringing back to Himself, according to the eternal vision He has for this redeemed creation.

God Wanted to Show the Man Where He (God) Was and Where He (the Man) Wasn't

Since God knows everything (Psalm 139), He wasn't actually unaware of where Adam was. He just wanted the man to know that something in their relationship had changed. The man reveals his position by his answer to God: "I heard . . . I was afraid . . . I was naked . . . I hid myself" (Genesis 3:10). How ironic! The one who prophesied the connectivity of husband and wife is now separating himself from his wife. He makes the first statement of masculinity but also makes the first statement of emasculation and selfishness. God's question to the first man is the same one He asks us. His purpose is to draw us out of our hiding places and to bring us to Him. Just as the leaf that Adam used to cover himself died as soon as he removed it from the vine, so man began to die as soon as he separated himself from God.

Thuggism. This is an exaggerated form of manhood that uses the smoke screen of anger and intimidation to keep people at a distance. The attitudes and behaviors associated with thuggism are all present in thug life. A word coined by the late Tupac Shakur, *thug* is often mistakenly thought to mean "criminal." Thug life is the opposite of someone having all he needs to succeed. Thug life is when you have nothing, yet still succeed, when you have overcome all obstacles to reach your aim. As pretty as many have tried to paint it, and as many excuses as have been made for its existence, thuggism has been one of the most influential forms of manhood training for many men. Having the "cred" of the block, the resources of a CEO, the eye of the ladies, and the envy of haters is the mark of the thug. It is not just about survival but is a commitment to not seeing beyond where you are now. Even though many have denigrated the thug life, it is a sign of its influence that it still lingers today as an image of manhood. At its core is survival without direction.

Grandmothers. Whether you call her Big Mama, Madea, Nana, Sugar Mama, or Granny, the grandmother has been the default leader in many black families all over the country. This transcends the urban context and finds its reality in rural areas also.

In the days of slavery and then of sharecropping, when black men generally were unable to achieve economic independence, the black grandmother was often a heroic figure whose role required great sacrifice. The black man was frequently, but not always, emasculated, weakened, or simply neutralized by the social control efforts of the wider white society and was thus reduced as a competitive force in a male-dominated society. But the black woman was not usually perceived to be as much of a threat to the dominance of the white man as the black man was. According to folklore, such women were allowed to develop into strong, independent, willful, and wise matriarchs who were not afraid to compete with men when necessary.

As in the past, the heroic grandmother will come to the aid of the family, taking responsibility for children abandoned by their own parents, asserting her considerable moral authority for the good of the family, and often rearing the children herself under conditions of great hardship.

The grandmother's central role has become institutionalized in the black community and carries with it a great deal of prestige, but also a great deal of stress. However, because this role is imbued with such prestige and moral authority and is so firmly entrenched in the culture, many of those who assume it see it as highly important, if not essential, for the survival of the black inner-city family.

A review of the literature on grandparenthood reveals that the existence of the institutionalized grandmother role is a major feature of black family life, particularly among the poor. Among inner-city blacks, this strong tradition is often seen as a mandatory role with established rights, obligations, and duties, and those who refuse it may be judged by many in the local black community as having abdicated a vital responsibility. Hence, when called upon, black grandmothers appear constrained to play out their role.[6]

This role became both a blessing and a curse. Despite its many benefits, the cycle of grandmothers becoming midwives, elders, and chiefs of families and neighborhoods has crippled masculinity. She became an icon for inner-city leadership in the family. With her status at platinum, it was a challenge for black men to realistically understand and accomplish their rightful role. Also she became a scapegoat for the willful negligence of youth and adults alike, receiving blame for acts and choices in which she was not involved. There needs to be a ceremony in which the grandmothers of the world transfer their authority back to men who are willing to use the mantle wisely and will take responsibility to conduct themselves in a biblical and comprehensive manner (Matthew 28:18–20; 2 Timothy 2:2).

God Was Willing to Go after the Man

When God looks for Adam in the garden, we see firsthand the missionary flare of the living God. He seeks out man while man hides from Him. While we are hiding, He calls to us too. Amidst our insecurities, challenges, and failures, He bids us to come.

---

[6]Elijah Anderson, *Code of the Street: Decency, Violence, and the Moral Life* (New York: W. W. Norton and Company, 1999).

TOWARD A BASIC BIBLICAL THEOLOGY OF MANHOOD

Before we define manhood, we must give a basic biblical portrait of manhood. For the most part, the Bible does not define what a man is, but it does give vivid portraits of manhood and characteristics of masculinity. We will not explore all of them, but we will go through a brief overview of these portraits. They are more powerful than any mere Western, linear definition of manhood. It is impossible to talk about masculinity without speaking of Genesis 1:26–28. These verses are highly controversial, but everything is clear in one respect—masculinity and femininity are distinct:

> Then God said, "Let us make man in our image, after our likeness. And let them have dominion over the fish of the sea and over the birds of the heavens and over the livestock and over all the earth and over every creeping thing that creeps on the earth."
>
> So God created man in his own image,
>   in the image of God he created him;
>   male and female he created them. (Genesis 1:26–27)

Manhood and womanhood are distinct and different but should be unified in their goal—the reflection of the One who created them. Mankind's being created in the likeness and image of God is a unified reality for both genders, but created men and women have distinct yet complementary ways in which to reveal that reality. We see God putting man in the garden to work (Genesis 2:15), we see God giving man great freedom and clear boundaries (Genesis 2:16–17), we see God bringing all the animals of the earth to man to name and legislating and affirming his name choice (Genesis 2:19), and we see God giving man a mate (Genesis 2:21–22). This mate is given in the context of man's naming God's sentient creation. Adam noticed from a physiological standpoint that he and the other parts of God's creation were different. However, the difference did not repel him; it drew him to preach and prophesy (Genesis 2:23–25). The woman is a co-equal reflector of the glory of God and is called to use her femininity to complete God's goal for relative self-replication of His image through mankind. It is man, however, who is called to lead this effort.

Man must lead God's creation in reflecting and replicating God's image. But after the fall, man began to replicate his own image (Genesis 6) among God's creation. However, God promised after the fall that He would appoint the seed of the woman to be a redeemer (Genesis 3:15). This redeemer is Jesus, who is the image of God untainted by sin (Colossians 1:15). Jesus became incarnate to show us who the Father is and what He looks like (Hebrews 1:3). The Lord Jesus therefore is the seed of Eve, yet He is different (John 1:18). He is perfectly able to reflect the image of God and also to replicate it. The cross is the center of God's replication strategy. Jesus gives His life to put man back in right relationship with God. As an application of that rightness, manhood is restored to its proper function through the cross (Colossians 1:20–22).

Romans 5:17 points to Jesus as the embodiment of what it means to be the new Man. The first man (Adam) flunked, but the second Man (the second Adam, Jesus) graduated with honors. Jesus as the new Man is the prototype for all that He died to redeem, and manhood is being restored by being conformed to the image of God, following the example set by Christ (Romans 8:29). To be conformed to Jesus's image automatically reconstructs man into God's image.

God the Father affirms Jesus as His Man and the Man that men should follow. God had not publicly spoken from heaven in public since Exodus 20:18–21. However, this was a special occasion, to put it mildly. Thus God says, "This is my beloved Son, with whom I am well pleased" (Matthew 3:17). At Jesus' introduction as Messianic King when He is baptized, God as a faithful Father shows up to affirm His Son, as well as to reveal His presence. Later on God does the same thing, affirming Jesus as His man to the disciples, as "a bright cloud overshadowed them, and a voice from the cloud said, 'This is my beloved Son, with whom I am well pleased; listen to him'" (Matthew 17:5). God lets man know His pleasure with His Son.

KEY CHARACTERISTICS OF BIBLICAL MANHOOD

An Initiator

Robert Lewis in his *Quest for Authentic Manhood* curriculum states, "Manhood is the willingness to take the initiative for the benefits of others." Taking the initiative is at the center of our Lord Jesus's philosophy of life. Although He saw Himself as sent, He was (and is) also an initiator of what God commanded Him. One of the challenges of manhood in today's society is passivity. Many view passivity as a characteristic of the soft man. Think of the nerdy dude who wears glasses and high-water pants and is timid around females. However, timidity in the Bible is defined a little differently. It is an unwillingness to execute God-centered mandates. Second Timothy 1:7 states, "For God gave us a spirit not of fear but of power and love and self-control." In context, Paul wants Timothy to walk in God's affirmed gifting and to receive the consequences (positive or negative) of reflecting who God has uniquely bred him to be as a man. In addition, he calls him to be courageous in the gospel (v. 8).

First Timothy 2:8 speaks of men being spiritual initiators. Men are supposed to initiate prayer and worship. Paul makes this a universal axiom. Nothing makes me more angry than to ask for someone to pray and have women respond first. Husky, raspy, and passionate voices of men should answer that call.

Worship in the African-American context has become an extremely feminine phenomenon. Expressions of worship often are feminine in nature. Men are often repelled by worship and do not feel the freedom to engage in it. The cultural feminization of worship has come from the absence of men as the initiators of worship. Therefore, we must return to our theological roots. Men must be present and ready to give Jesus his due in public and private gatherings.

Moreover, a famine also exists in homes where men are absent and where men who are present still seem absent. Men are supposed to initiate spirituality in the home. Ephesians 5:26, 29 points to this. Men are to initiate biblical and theological vitality in the home. Jesus confronts the church about her spiritual needs (Revelation 1–3). Jesus does not merely wait for the church to come and tell Him what she needs. Jesus's masculinity patrols the church to inspect and challenge her progress (Revelation 2:1). However, He does it in a way that is nourishing and cherishing. He does not abuse the church in His leading but keeps her safe and protected from evil.

Gospel Courage

Gospel courage is the willingness to be faithful to the gospel in life despite the negative reactions that may come from other men, looking instead to God and His blessing (Romans 1:16). Men must be willing to fill all of their life with the truth of the gospel. Dying to evil is the gateway into gospel-centered living for the Christian. Jesus's death is the gateway into all that God has for creation (2 Corinthians 5:17–21; Colossians 1:19–20). We must have the courage to die, just as Christ did.

Paul speaks of his positional and practical death experience(s). He speaks of the courage necessary to identify with Jesus at the expense of himself (Acts 16; Philippians 1:12–30). This is manhood at its best. The picture of dying to gain Christ is prevalent in Philippians 1:20–21. Pressing on, suffering, and loss are expressions of pain and struggle, but the result is a blessing, the gaining of Jesus and true manhood.

Speaking into the Future of Men

One of the greatest manhood chapters in the Bible is Genesis 49. Jacob, nearing death, called his sons to himself. It is a practice that he had received from his dad Isaac (Genesis 27). In this passage Jacob shows his vast knowledge of his sons' wiring, actions, and spiritual capacity. He warns them, challenges them, encourages them, speaks prophetically to them, and prays over them. His display is God-initiated, and God uses his raising of his sons and his interaction with them as a pipeline for His words.

Jacob, with all of his issues, was a dad who was around. His presence is reflected in his intimate understanding of the lives of his sons. Some of what he said was very blunt, but it was needed for such a rambunctious crew. He calls Reuben "unstable" and calls Simeon and Levi hotheaded. He calls Judah a king, Zebulun a beach boy, Issachar a "donkey," Dan a judge and a snake, Asher an enjoyer of rich foods, Naphtali a free doe, and Joseph "fruitful." Men having an intimate knowledge of their sons are rare. In order to develop men, we must be with them, understand them, and have the courage to challenge them.

Every man knows that even though we all have massive egos that are easily bruised, the wounds inflicted by well-meaning, key men in our lives are deeply valued. Men, like Jesus, who regularly rebuke and encourage are needed. Jesus struck an amazing balance between these two actions. He challenged Peter's youthful zeal in making emotional commitments, knowing that Peter would not follow through on his promise (John 13:38), but still encouraged him after his fall (Luke 22:31–32; John 21:15–19).

Setting Men up to Win

In 1 Chronicles 22:2–19 we see a dad displaying an intimate understanding of his son and the role he must play as a father to set up his son for success. David was told by God that he would not build the temple. As passionate as David was about this, he submitted to the Lord in this matter. The Lord told him that his son would have the honor instead. Although David may have been disappointed, he was man enough to make sure that his son was prepared to succeed in the plans that the Lord had for him.

Since the Lord stated that it was Solomon who would build the temple, David wanted to make sure that his son had everything set in place for this work to occur in a way that would glorify God. Therefore David used his knowledge of his son and his sphere of influence to aid in the process. He states in verse 5, "Solomon my son is young and inexperienced." This statement is not spoken out of envy of the role Solomon would play in David's stead but shows a real understanding of where his son was lacking. Solomon himself would later acknowledge his lack of wisdom to the Lord. In light of Solomon's youth and inexperience, David states, "'I will therefore make preparation for it.' So David provided materials in great quantity before his death." The king viewed his role as helping his son win, all for the glory of God.

In this powerful statement we see that David had such a passion for God's glory that he prepared his son to fulfill his role in glorifying God. David stated, "The house that is to be built for the LORD must be exceedingly magnificent, of fame and glory throughout all lands." His concern for how God is viewed motivated him to alley-oop the legacy to his son through giving him the resources he would need.

Men prepare other men and give them the resources to glorify God. One of the greatest faults among black men is a lack of passion to see younger men win. Many will state a passion for this, but rarely do we see a sufficient level of effort by black men to establish an environment for winning. Developing a winning environment is of great importance for every man. I am a church planter, and 98 percent of the support that we have received was from non-African-Americans. One pastor stated, "You have more than I had at the point in which you are currently, so I figure you need to struggle like I did. A part of your learning is earning." It blew my mind that he believed he was setting me up to win by giving me as little as possible. He assumed that if resources were given to me, it would make me inadequate, as if the giver thought I wasn't strong enough to do it on my own. But in actuality we should want the men who come after us to bring Jesus more glory than we did. We should want them to be more gifted, more talented, more intellectually astute, more emotionally connected to their wives, more influential, more effective providers, better dads, etc. As time goes on, we should see the abundant lives of those who have gone before us fill the next generation with more abundance. Jesus's passion is that His disciples would reach more people with their ministry than He did (John 14:12). He sets them up to win, even in His ascension to heaven.

So many young men in the Hip-Hop/Eclectic Generation feel extremely frustrated and unfathered. Most of the men I shepherd deal with deep daddy deprivation. This deprivation has created spiritual blind spots that set up booby traps along their road to sanctification. The worst of them all is the façade or mask that young men use to deceive people with whom they come in contact into thinking that they are all right. Examples include theological knowledge void of spiritual formation or comedic relief that aids them in not being taken seriously. Older black Christian men must be able to see beyond that fog, like David, and speak into the life of a young man in light of his chronic weaknesses. Solomon's weaknesses did not demotivate David but drove him to be a loving resource to his son, so Solomon could bring maximum glory to God.

KEYS TO DEVELOPING MASCULINE MEN

Ability to Use Resources Wisely

Stewardship means to oversee what has been placed within your sphere or under your charge, thereby maximizing its use for the owner's benefit while it is in your possession. The Bible speaks often of this idea. In Luke 16:1–8 Jesus tells a story about a shrewd manager. Ultimately Jesus wanted God's people to understand how to use God's resources to the advantage of the kingdom. In black culture we speak with one another about what we assume whites teach their children. We assume that whites keep this info for "their own kind" on subjects like money, property, and education. We feel like there is a secret system that white people have to ensure they are better than anyone else. There is a sense of inferiority among blacks, as if our ability to maximize what Jesus has placed under our charge will always be limited. The truth is that our ability as black people to maximize what Jesus has placed under our charge is dependent on God's provision and our ability to embrace godly principles regarding working, spending, saving, and so on.

Able to Emotionally Connect

"We don't love dem hoes" is a colloquialism developed by Snoop Dogg and affirmed by men about the need to maintain emotional distance from women. Jay-Z on *The Blueprint* had a hit song that spoke of "girls, girls, girls, all over the world." He speaks throughout the video in a nonchalant way about how connected and into him the girls were, but how disconnected he was from them. We could go on to gangster rhymes that speak of emotional disconnect from authority or 50 Cent speaking of killing another man and being emotionally disconnected from any sort of remorse.

These and many other examples of emotional disconnect have become staples of unredeemed manhood. To be a distant man has become accepted—and even encouraged! Being emotionally invested in anything but your favorite sports teams, the neighborhood you grew up in, white AF1's, and new Timberland boots is unacceptable. But it's okay to be emotionally vested in the woman all the dudes want but only you have. This is because the attachment is self-centered. Some of these issues are generalizations; yet they are embedded on some level in the psyche of almost every black dude who is not a social outcast.

The Bible teaches that God wants worship from every fabric of our being, from both men and women (Mark 12:29–31). God wants all of humanity to worship Him. Man was made to love God with his whole being. Although this has been defaced by the fall, Jesus died to make it possible for us to holistically love God again. God made the first move through Jesus, demonstrating His love for us before we would move toward Him (Romans 5:8). God created us with intellect, emotions, and volition. Since that is a part of who we are, we must use everything within our being as instruments of worship (Colossians 1:20). Men must be taught the skill of emotional connection through the example of Jesus Christ.

Men must be connected with God again in order to apply this reality from a redemptive standpoint. Then men must acknowledge and resolve the pains of their past. Although Paul states in

Philippians 3:13 that we should be "forgetting what lies behind [us]," we must first acknowledge the existence of that past in order to give it to Jesus.

Peter Scazzero profoundly lists several problems contributing to emotional unhealthiness:

• Ignoring the emotions of anger, sadness, and fear
• Dying to the wrong things
• Denying the past's impact on the present
• Covering over brokenness, weaknesses, and failure
• Living without limits[7]

For most of us men, our lack of emotional connectivity can be dated back to some event we would like to forget. It also does not help that black folks, especially dudes, do not affirm the role of counseling in their lives. The pattern of pretending to be okay when you really are not needs to stop. Time does not fix brokenness; skillful application of the gospel does. If we reconnect broken men with the gospel's healing power, there will be a greater level of health in marriage, friendships, parenting, church community, missional engagement of one's context, and spiritual formation. All of these benefits are on hold until we men are able to face God and their past.

Able to Reproduce Properly and Purposefully—
Spiritual Reproduction

Black Christian men must understand that they cannot both live the Christian life and not strive to reproduce solid disciples of Jesus Christ. Matthew 28:18–20 is a call to everyone in the church, not just the pastor. It is a shame that many of us as black pastors are so insecure and timid that we view men engaging other men and creating disciples of Christ within the local church as competition with our spiritual authority. Pastors must see this as an extension

---

[7]Peter Scazzero, *Emotionally Healthy Spirituality: Unleash the Power of Life in Christ* (Nashville: Integrity Publishers, 2006), 24.

of their spiritual work and a great win for Christ, who is "the chief Shepherd" (1 Peter 5:4).

Any pastor who wants to see God work in the lives of men must have a healthy view of spiritual reproduction. Making disciples, leading a small group, communicating with and rallying people, or being called to plant a church is a death wish for many young men who are in the church today. They know too well that the pastor will be saddened not because he will miss being around them if they leave or because they will not be as connected to him relationally, but because he believes that enabling them to lead will breed competition. Yes, sometimes you get hurt, even by those who into whom you have poured your life—that is a part of leadership. This is revealed in Scripture and is normal. That is why Paul urges us to maximize our time with the faithful (2 Timothy 2:2). The only other option is what has been called controlled empowerment—when a pastor releases someone, but only with a leash still attached.

Our course of action must be for men to reproduce godly men through discipleship. Spending His life on the faithful was Jesus's passion, and this must be a shared passion of ours. In fact, it is a command. We do not need a key program to practice discipleship—we must just start it. We must make disciples beyond the men's ministry. It must be an organic culture of the church. The leadership should have fewer speaking engagements and spend more time with small groups of the faithful. Meeting with younger men, we can go through character studies on manhood in the Bible or books written on gospel-centered manhood and/or bring them along with us during a natural part of our week and show them biblical manhood in action.

Physical Reproduction

In Philadelphia a former mayor stated that 90 percent of the children born in Philly were born to single-parent homes. This is a pandemic! Philly is 45 percent black, and this statistic is true of our populace. Men need to be engaged with the gospel. We must target men. One of the many problems facing the black community today is that we do not have a problem reproducing, but much of it is done illegitimately. Jesus wants legitimate reproduction. In order to engage men, we must inspire manliness in the culture of the church. Flowers all around the pulpit, ladies choosing the colors for where the saints gather, and feminine men are the dominant visual. We can have all the social justice programs we want—cool cats will come to that stuff during the week for a handout, and even a hand up, but they will still remain wary of Christianity and the gospel. Once men are engaged, they must see the raising up of godly disciples of Christ as an indigenous Christian trait for men (Proverbs 1). The raising of godly men will end the cycle. Raising solid Christian children will give people in the next generation a new past (Psalm 102:18). Hopefully they won't have to get over our view of Christianity in order to become children of the Father.

6

THE CHURCH AND COMMUNITY

Lance Lewis

"Our playgrounds have become battlegrounds. Our streets have become cemeteries. Our schools have become places to mourn the ones we've lost." Those were the words of then Senator Barack Obama in July 2007 after the particularly brutal murder of sixteen-year-old Blair Holt in the city of Chicago. And as sad and shocking as that was, it was not the last murder of a young black person by his peers that caused the collective African-American community to reflect on where we are and to wonder what's going on.

Within a year of President Obama's improbable election, Derrion Albert was brutally and mercilessly beaten to death while on his way home from school in the very same city where President-elect Obama gave his historical acceptance speech. How could this happen? How is it that over fifty years after *Brown v. Board of Education* and in the wake of the first elected African-American president of our country that still too often our playgrounds have become battlegrounds, streets have become cemeteries, and schools have become places to mourn the ones we've lost?

THE PROBLEM

There is much talk, discussion, musing, and writing about what African-Americans should do now. What steps ought we to take to finally address and reverse the social ills and pathologies that have plagued and worked against us? And the position and place of the black church is never far from these discussions. Most of those who discuss these things believe that the church has some role to play, but that role is not one of cultural transformation. Instead, it is said, the church is relegated to the role of volunteer social service agency. We are to be among those who step in and assist our communities in coping with the pathologies and who are part of the glue that holds our neighborhoods together. Rarely, if ever, are we asked to take a peek at the root causes of those pathologies and speak to them. And even more rarely are we asked to encourage our people to lift their gaze from this world to the world to come. We want the church to be the prophetic voice in our community as long as that voice is aimed at those outside the church who oppress us or those within it who oppose us. Even when we call our people to behave rightly, we are not supposed to tie it to the obedience we owe to our Creator but rather should call for it because behaving rightly makes better social sense than behaving irresponsibly.

Likewise, we want the church to be the visionary of our people as long as that vision is confined to our apprehension of the American dream and leaves out any kind of pie-in-the-sky talk of some far-off new heaven and earth. We want our pie now, and we intend to enjoy it however we please.

Most of us know how we came to view the church this way. The trauma of perpetual ethnic enslavement and subsequent marginalization to barely second-class citizenry created a profound and lasting impression on the psyche, emotions, and souls of black folks. There is no need to bore you with statistics or to attempt to shock you with actual horror stories. We all know the stats and have heard the stories. Against the backdrop of incredible dehumanization, the black church stood as the one foundational rock of black humanity.

As my brother Carl Ellis Jr. says, "You may have worked as a janitor and been called john and 'boy' all week long, but in church you were Deacon Jones." Black people and the black community came to rely on the church as the main agent and actor in our ongoing quest to be simply regarded as people created in God's image and thus owed a measure of dignity, respect, kindness, and justice.

The church was viewed with respect as a community of people

who looked out for the interests of black people. Moreover, though she did not do it perfectly, the church stood as an example of the life of godliness that those created in God's image were to embody. The black church was also instrumental in the civil rights struggle. Led by the black church, the black community sustained a multi-decade, peaceful revolution that succeeded in ending entrenched, legalized segregation and discrimination. In effect the church breached the walls of a century of accepted social practice and effectively opened a crack in the door of opportunity for subsequent generations of black folks.

But a crack is about all we could expect the church to muster. It would be up to the gatekeepers of American opportunity and social mobility to open the door wide to genuine ethnic unity and integration, a door they simply were not prepared to open. Thus, while black folks could now legally ride in the front of the bus, it was more often than not still a trip to nowhere. The North and Midwest had long proved that African-Americans could effectively be shut out of the opportunities afforded to the newest European immigrant to America, and this without the need for overt Jim Crow laws. Consequently, as we slid into the 1970s we black folks found ourselves in a situation in which we were tolerated but not welcome. We were admitted but not necessarily accepted. Though the government declared war on poverty, it was more like a proxy war than an actual effort to permanently lift black people out of poverty. So while the government continued to promote social and fiscal policies that enabled wealth to concentrate in the country's new suburban enclaves, black people and the cities in which they lived had to settle for leftover handouts of stale government cheese, butter, and hope. That was the first unforeseen consequence of the civil rights struggle that the African-American community was unprepared to handle. How do you fight against an enemy that smiles in your face and tells you all is well but still holds tightly the reins of power, wealth, and opportunity and then blames you for not getting with the program?

This is the situation in which black people and the black church found themselves throughout the seventies and into Reagan's eighties. And it is that circumstance that may have contributed directly to the second consequence of the civil rights movement. Langston Hughes once wrote:

What happens to a dream deferred?
Does it dry up
like a raisin in the sun?
Or fester like a sore—
And then run?
Does it stink like rotten meat?
Or crust and sugar over—
like a syrupy sweet?
Maybe it just sags
like a heavy load.
Or does it explode?[1]

I would say that by the time the black community limped into the mid-to-late eighties, our dreams for an integrated society in which we would be authentically judged by the content of our character exploded, sending the shrapnel of hopelessness and despair deep into our communities. Looking at many African-American communities in 1988 would cause one to genuinely wonder if we were better off in 1958. This was the atmosphere within black America when Bill Cosby addressed the NAACP on the fiftieth anniversary of *Brown v. Board of Education* in Constitution Hall in Washington, DC on May 17, 2004 and declared, "What . . . good is *Brown v. Board of Education* if nobody wants it?"

What had happened, and how did things so quickly deteriorate in the ways we African-Americans thought of ourselves, our challenges, this world, and our place within it? At some point, and I cannot say exactly when, a segment of our community accepted, embraced, promoted, and glorified the very dehumanization against which the civil rights movement fought so long and so

---

[1]See http://www.americanpoems.com/poets/Langston-Hughes/2381.

bravely. In so doing, they effectively redefined blackness in terms of nihilism, perpetual victimization, and underachievement. This idea of blackness was recorded, packaged, marketed, and then sold to the masses as the only blackness that mattered. And if you question whether this became the entrenched notion of modern blackness, just ask yourself who most African-Americans thought was more authentically black in the beginning of 2006—Barack Obama or 50 Cent?

By the time the Democrats finally regained the White House in the early nineties, the African-American community (and the black church) found itself in a war with two fronts. On one side America was still a racialized (though not racist) society in that the economic, social, psychological, and emotional benefits of the country were still weighted toward the dominant ethnicity. On the other side a significant aspect of the greater black community had deteriorated to the point where one wondered if African-Americans longed to remain in the permanent underclass as much as their forebears had longed to end segregation and take their place in America. And it was not as if this new black attitude was just confined to those with a dependent income level. In his series of essays entitled *What's Going On*, author Nathan McCall wrote about this attitude in the chapter "Faking the Funk: The Black Middle Class of Prince Georges County." McCall noted how the children of well-educated, middle- and upper-class black people lustily gobbled up the culture of underachievement, negativity, disrespect, and instant gratification.

The black church now finds itself in a two-front war with no real idea of how to engage either front. But *could* the church have foreseen this turn of attitude among black folks? Black people had lived closely enough among whites to see whites' private depravity up close and personal. We knew firsthand that wealth, power, opportunity, and social status does not prevent people from acting on their all-too-human desires. As Rev. Howard Brown says, "If Ward and June really had it together in the 50s, their children

wouldn't have been wilding out at Woodstock in the 60s." We saw
and therefore could have known that just because you could hide
immorality behind stately homes, superior education, growing
economies, and well-thought-out theology articulated in well-run
churches doesn't mean that immorality is not present. We might
have seen that the white evangelical church had failed its community, with disastrous consequences. And I'm not just referring to the
catastrophic failure of evangelical theology to impact the way that
the evangelical church and community responded to a society built
upon and determined to maintain white supremacy. It was their
innate belief that the blessings of their society must mean that God
was on their side that led them to turn a blind eye to the gross immorality that lived within their homes, represented their interests in the
halls of Congress, and worshiped with them on Sunday mornings.
How did the evangelical church fail the dominant society? They did
so by tribalizing the living God.

THE SOLUTION

What do I mean by *tribalizing God*? To tribalize God is to preach,
teach, and live as though He exists to promote the narrow interest
of a particular group, culture, or country. All cultures do this to
some extent or another, which is why it is important for the black
church to resist the urge to do so now. Cultures that tribalize God
always fail to take Him seriously enough to deal with their own sin
issues. This helps answer the question of how Reformed churches
in particular could on the one hand affirm that God's choice to save
individuals has nothing to do with any positive traits or characteristics arising from those individuals while on the other hand denying
Communion to confessing believers solely on the basis of skin color.
They, like their evangelical brethren, gave in to a form of the social
gospel by putting the sinful social desires of their culture above the
godly eternal truths of Scripture. They failed by not confronting
and challenging their communities to embrace Christ authentically
and live out the implications of His gospel fully. They were willing

to enjoy the privileges that God's sovereignty brought them without ever reflecting on the reason behind those blessings. They muted God and relegated Him to the status of divine mascot.

As I stated previously, that is a perfectly understandable way for countries, cultures, and peoples to view God. Despite the radical secularism of the West most of the world is still deeply religious, with much of that religious effort aimed at securing the favor of a particular deity for the purpose of enjoying the advantages of wealth, opportunity, security, and wholeness in the here and now. The problem when you encounter the God of Scripture, however, is that He has His own agenda and refuses to be tribalized. He will not be used or prostituted to carry out the will of a particular country or people group. He cannot be tamed, will not be bribed, would never allow Himself to be bought, and is so utterly complete and sufficient within Himself that He really does not need any of us for anything. Any country or people group that dares view Him as their own private tribal warrior who exists mainly to do their bidding and deliver the goods runs the risk of watching their country or people group crumble in successive cycles of destructive depravity even as they rise to the top of the social food chain.

The challenge for the twenty-first-century black church is that it is exactly what our community would expect of us. They would expect the church to put all of its resources, energy, and effort into facilitating our long climb from the bottom of the well. The danger for the black church is that we could do just that. We could spend the next few decades completely refocusing our mission, pour out of our buildings and into our communities, and tackle all the issues and pathologies that have plagued us since being brought to these shores from Africa. Please do not misunderstand me. The church should be active in addressing the issues with which our people struggle. But if all we do is join the chorus to relieve our distress, then at most we might succeed in reforming our people and communities. However, the subject of this chapter is *transforming* our communities and culture. And we will not effectively work toward community and cultural transformation if all we settle for is our place at the table and our slice of the American pie.

What then ought the church to do and teach so that by God's grace and power we might see genuine community and cultural transformation? What message should we deliver to our people so that by His grace we might have a godly effect not only on our communities but also on America and perhaps on the world itself? We must cultivate a *desire* for a satisfaction greater than the life of prosperity, comfort, and convenience in the American dream, be *devoted* to a mission more significant and permanent than lifting black folks from the underclass into the middle class, and *determine* to seek a place more beautiful, pristine, bountiful, and secure than the suburbs of our major cities.

Where do we begin? The same place Jesus did when He launched a ministry that would eventually transform a people who would transform the world. Jesus once spoke to a community of people very much like ours. Like us, these people lived as a subdominant group in a society in which the economic, political, emotional, and psychological benefits were weighted toward the dominant society. Like us, these people held to a strong belief in God, with the corresponding belief that God would come to their aid against their enemies. Like us, these people believed that the foreign dominant society was their chief obstacle to the life they really wanted to live, and like all subdominant people groups, they bore the scars of their second-class citizenship. And finally, like us, these people were eager to listen to anyone who gave any hint of once and for all dealing with the dominant society and bringing his people back to prominence. Jesus Christ was just such a person. Here was a man who spoke for God, stood apart from the existing religious establishment, and did authentic miracles to back up His new teaching. Surely He would be the one who would lead the great Jewish revolt that would once for all throw off Roman rule and reestablish King David's dynasty. Or would He?

Eventually and to their own disappointment, the masses would find that Jesus was much more radical and revolutionary than they bargained for. We too tend to think that Jesus was revolutionary because He sided with the poor and less powerful against the rich and powerful. But that is not the essence or even foundation of His teaching. What made Jesus's teaching far more revolutionary than His people wanted then and we believe now is how that teaching *prepared His followers to transform this world by focusing their minds and affections on the world to come.*

To put it another way, Jesus taught that His followers should *desire* an otherworldly satisfaction, *devote* themselves to a mission more significant than lifting the temporary fortunes of their people, and *determine* to seek a place more beautiful, peaceful, just, secure, and loving than any place this world has to offer. In what ways did the Lord's teaching do this, and how can it guide us in the quest to transform our communities? Let's begin by considering an overview of the Sermon on the Mount, one of His most important messages. The first part of Jesus's teaching in this message is commonly referred to as the Beatitudes. They are called that because each saying is preceded by a word translated "blessed." What does it mean to be blessed in this sense? It means to enjoy God's special, unmerited favor that ultimately results in having a strong desire to love, know, delight in, and enjoy God as an end in and of itself. In other words, those who are blessed in the biblical sense are blessed because above all things their chief desire is to enjoy the soul satisfaction that only comes through a worshiping relationship with God through Jesus Christ. In fact, the very first beatitude ("Blessed are the poor in spirit, for theirs is the kingdom of heaven," Matthew 5:3) captures that sentiment perfectly. "The poor in spirit" are "blessed" because by God's grace they have realized that only a worshiping relationship with the living God through Jesus Christ can deliver the authentic soul satisfaction everyone else craves. Our people and communities will never ultimately find satisfaction in an American dream no matter how much prosperity, comfort, and convenience it delivers. All of the money, social respect, and upward mobility that we could ever gain will mean nothing apart from a thriving, worshipping relationship with our Creator.

How could a deep desire for a vital, worshiping relationship with God through Jesus Christ transform our people, culture, and communities? A look at the rest of the Beatitudes reveals that once an individual, family, community, and culture settles for nothing less than soul satisfaction, they are prepared to take on the world. Why? Because they have been freed from having to wear themselves out chasing the mirages of worldly satisfaction that are as fleeting as the summer's morning mist. Such a person or culture is then able to seek satisfaction in pursuing the agenda of his or her Creator-King, which involves spreading His love, grace, holiness, peace, justice, hope, knowledge, righteousness, and worship for His glory and *for the good of those impacted by His influence through His people.*

We move from seeking satisfaction in something other than this world to devoting ourselves to a mission more significant than raising the temporary fortunes of our people. This is another place where Jesus is far more revolutionary and radical than we commonly think. The key to that mission is found in the beatitude in which Jesus declared that one of the characteristics of the blessed ones is their willingness to endure rejection and intolerance because of who He is and what He came to do. By the time we come to the end of Matthew's Gospel we find that Jesus's mission had nothing to do with raising the temporary fortunes of the Jewish people. Instead His mission involved living a sinless life, dying a sacrificial death, and physically rising again from the dead to satisfy fully God's standard of righteousness and justice and so pay for the sins of God's people. That is the springboard for the mission Jesus gave to His closest followers, which involves spreading godliness throughout the world by working to make active followers of Christ among people of all ethnicities.

This highlights the reality that Christ's stated mission for His church is cultural transformation to the extent that whole people groups reorient their existence around obeying, worshiping, serving, loving, and delighting in the living God through a worshiping relationship with Jesus Christ. Embracing this mission will move us from the notion that maintaining the military, political, and economic dominance of the United States is somehow God's will or must at least be a part of His plan. It also affirms the truth that it is not His express will to raise black folks into the middle income levels of American society so they can enjoy the "blessings of liberty." Finally, we must grasp the truth that we can no longer regard the black church as *our* black church simply on the basis that it arose from our shared history and struggle, so that we now shape its content, mission, and direction for the temporal fortunes of our people. Rather, the black church is black to the extent that it calls black people to drop their African-American idols, take up the cross of Jesus Christ, and become active followers of Jesus Christ.

How will devotion to a mission more significant than lifting the temporary fortunes of our people transform our communities and culture? Once again let us look at some passages from the Beatitudes. After declaring that His followers would endure hardships, Jesus went on to say that those same followers would spend their lives exerting a positive godly impact on their communities and culture (see Matthew 5:13–16). They will do this by engaging in face-to-face, life-on-life contact with those in their communities and by using their talents, abilities, and acquired skills to build up the quality of life for those communities. They will do this in pursuit of their primary mission—to spread godliness throughout the world by declaring the gospel and making active followers of Jesus Christ.

We conclude our short homily on transformation by calling our people to long for a place more beautiful, peaceful, righteous, secure, and loving than any place this world has to offer. This is where the radical nature of Jesus's teaching obliterates our preconceived notions about who He is and what He came to do. Take another look at the Sermon on the Mount, and note how many times Jesus refers to "the kingdom of heaven." What does He mean by this phrase? The kingdom of heaven is the express, purposeful rule and reign of the living God over all His creation for His own glory and our good. The essence of the kingdom is the worship of the King, Jesus Christ, and the pursuit and establishment of His rule, word, peace, gospel, and service. The kingdom has both a *now* and *not yet* dimension. It exists *now* in that Christ is the King, and His rule extends directly through His church, which consists of those who have been called by the Father, have been born again through the power of the Spirit, and have believed in the person and work of Jesus Christ for forgiveness of sin. The church is characterized by a group of people who orient their lives around the worship of God, an obedient walk before God, and an active witness for God. It exists *not yet* in that there is a point in time when Christ will rule from an actual new heaven and new earth. This rule will encompass every living being in the universe, will extend to every millimeter of the universe, and will never end. Moreover, the place of Christ's rule (the new heaven and new earth) will be the most glorious, beautiful, peace-filled, holy, righteous, loving, secure, fulfilling place that humanity will ever experience. And this is the place that we as God's church long for with all our heart and soul. Consequently we are determined to seek His rule in the here and now.

So how can a people so heavenly-minded possibly be of any earthly good?

Let us cast our eyes on a portion of the Sermon on the Mount, the last half of Matthew 6. It begins (v. 19) with Jesus's declaring, "Do not lay up for yourselves treasures on earth, where moth and rust destroy and where thieves break in and steal." Why do people spend their lives doing all they can to get as much as they can in the here and now? They do so because from their perspective the here and now is all there is. But here is the more probing question: how can those bent on seeking the lifestyles of the rich and famous ever make a real and lasting difference in their communities? On the other hand, how can those determined to make His rule their primary concern affect their communities? They can because having been freed from chasing the mythical, middle-class mirage they can reposition themselves to extend the blessings of the rule of the King to their communities and culture. In so doing they point those communities and culture to the return of the King and the glorious, eternal kingdom that will be the ultimate and permanent fulfillment of all their hope and longings.

THE WAY FORWARD

So where do we go from here? What must the church do to chart the way forward for our people?

We can begin by accepting that at root our challenges are theological and not sociological. That is not to say that our problems do not have sociological consequences—they do. What do I mean by saying that the root of our problem is theological? I mean that despite our outward religious veneer we are at war with God and are losing badly. We have disregarded His person, degraded His worship, disobeyed His Word, and dismissed His Son. And yes, I am talking about the church. Since the root of our problem is theological (that is, it lies in the way we misunderstand and thus misapprehend who He is and what He is about), we have no choice but to approach the solution from a theological vantage point. We can do this by making use of theological methods built on core biblical realities.

The first method that comes to mind is that of *gospel-driven prayer*. Gospel-driven prayer is prayer that prioritizes the expansion of the kingdom through the promotion of the gospel, which leads to individuals becoming active followers of Jesus Christ. It is prayer that joyfully embraces the blessed truth that we live for the glory of God. It's the kind of prayer that fills the Scriptures. What ought we to pray? Taking our lead from Scripture, we should pray that God would give those who believe in Christ a gnawing craving to know Him as an end in and of itself. We could pray that God's people would demonstrate that He is indeed and in fact more than enough to satisfy the longings of our souls. In line with that, we must pray that God's people would experience the living water promised by our Lord and Savior Jesus Christ. We must pray that this experience of genuine spiritual life through Christ alone will flood our souls to the extent that we are permanently weaned away from the hollow trinkets of this world.

Why the emphasis on prayer? Isn't prayer just a bit passive in light of our very real and present dangers? Prayer is essential because, among other things, prayer acknowledges that God and God alone can make the inward changes to the heart that result in lasting change. Engaging God in prayer admits that we lack the power, intellect, common sense, and will to make definitive lasting change. Prayer also accepts that God is at work in the world and in our people through Jesus Christ and by the power of the Holy Spirit for His glory. What do we mean by that? Simply that God acts so that once the goal is accomplished, we will recognize that it happened by His wisdom, power, goodness, grace, and knowledge for the express purpose of bringing individuals and groups of people to turn from sin and turn to Jesus Christ.

Our next weapon in this war for the souls of black folks is *the preaching of the Word of God*. Allow me to suggest a more scripturally consistent way for pastors to preach the Word and for participants to listen to the Word.

Few would argue with the rich preaching tradition of the black church. Fewer still would deny the emotional power of black preaching. My call is not for us to change the style of black preaching as much as it is to center our preaching squarely in the text of Scripture. This kind of preaching takes its cue from Scripture by allowing the text and themes of a particular passage to form the essence of the message. Pastors must pray and strive not necessarily to get a word from the Lord but to be empowered by the Spirit to faithfully preach the Word we have already been given. Our preaching must move from hit-or-miss topics aimed at speaking a word to our current life episodes to moving through the books and major themes of the Bible.

Why must our preaching change in this way?

Preaching through the books and major themes of the Bible is the most effective way to allow the text of Scripture to shape and form the essence of the message. This is crucial because faithful preaching through the texts of Scripture is the way we highlight and emphasize the character and nature of God as expressed fully in the person and work of Jesus Christ. And when the people of God hear and perceive the glory of God proclaimed through the tapestry of Scripture that culminates in the sinless life, sacrificial death, and glorious resurrection of Jesus Christ they get a vision of Him and not of themselves. They are lifted from an unhealthy concentration on their own issues and their desires to have their dreams fulfilled and are drawn to a godly focus on the grand vision of the living God, which is to fill His world with godliness. Seeing this vision as worked out in Scripture will move us to enlist in the mission of expanding His kingdom into our communities and culture. It is this vision of the glory of God, the saving gospel of His Son Jesus Christ, and the certain triumph of His eternal kingdom that we must take into our communities.

How are we to do this?

We take this message of cultural transformation into our communities by having the church cultivate a lifestyle of service for a lifetime. This simply means that every believer in Jesus Christ commits to setting aside regular time to engage his or her community by doing good using the abilities, skills, and talents he or she has. Followers of Christ view this aspect of their faith in much the same way they view attending regular worship, Bible study, choir practice, and men's and women's groups.

What steps can we take to begin to develop this dynamic? We have to begin by keeping the main thing the main thing. A heavenly mind-set is crucial if we wish to have churches that actually transform communities. The Sermon on the Mount is proof that those who are heavenly minded can make real and lasting change. They can do so because in Christ they've already been given all that brings authentic soul satisfaction, in Christ they've been given the greatest of all callings and missions, and in Christ they've been given a place in an eternal kingdom that is far more beautiful, righteous, peaceful, glorious, and wonderful than any neighborhood no matter how nice and well-kept in suburban America.

So where do we get started? I'm going to use one example of how a church can focus on a particular group of people within its area and effectively serve them as a way of bringing tangible, long-term transformation to their community. In this hypothetical example a local church will focus its energy on high-school teenagers aged fourteen through eighteen. Their goal is to provide a holistic youth ministry that will result in increasing the graduation and college acceptance rates at the neighborhood high school.

To begin, the church takes a comprehensive assessment of its members' talents, skills, acquired abilities, etc. This is not to be confused with their spiritual gifts. Instead these are abilities (e.g., painting) or acquired skills (e.g., carpentry). The goal is to generate a database of all available skills and talents that can be used to serve the youths and their families.

From there the church will reorganize how it spends its time and money. Concerning its time, they will have to transition one of their regular fellowship times (e.g., Wednesday evening Bible study) into a community focus night. This will be a time to work with the community teens and their families. The church can organize this night into a time of academic, social, cultural, and spiritual enrichment. For instance, the church could take that evening to prepare and serve a meal to the teens and their families followed by a presentation and discussion on various topics related to getting and staying in college. The church can also use this evening as a way of matching up community youths and their families with church members who will commit to praying for them on a regular basis.

Another way the church could serve community youths is by establishing a safe, organized place for teens to go immediately after school. The church could open its building to serve a healthy meal, provide a place to begin doing academic work, and even give individual counseling to those students who just wish to talk. In keeping with its commitment to the community youths, the church will invest some of its financial resources into hiring a full-time youth director responsible for directly engaging the youth and coordinating the church's ministry with those youths' parents/guardians and the school.

Since it's important to get as many members as possible involved in this ministry (assuming the church takes this on as its major community outreach), the congregation will also take a full survey of the parents/guardians of the youths it serves with the aim of having church members begin to use their skills to address the felt needs of these families.

This is just one possible way for a church to begin to effectively engage its community with a view to gospel-driven transformation. The overall goal is not confined to merely increasing the graduation rate of poor African-American students. The goal is to have the community see and closely observe a group of people who live for someone greater than themselves, serve a cause far more significant than helping their people obtain the middle-class mirage, and look forward to a place far more glorious than a 2,500-square-foot building in a quiet development in a cul-de-sac.

7

REDEEMED AND HEALED FOR MISSION

Anthony B. Bradley

Cornel West opens chapter 12 ("Wisdom") in the book *Hope on a Tightrope* with this sobering reality: "If you live long enough, a moment of spiritual death is inevitable. The question is: How will you deal with it?"[1] If there is a consensus among Cosby, Poussaint, and the authors of this book, it is this: people in trouble should actively seek help.[2] Because the themes of sin, brokenness, and redemption run through each of our lives, we stand poised to receive desperately needed help. In the black community, however, many are reluctant or unable to obtain the necessary help to heal their weary and wounded souls. For reasons that run the gamut from financial constraints to prideful avoidance, people who need help the most often do not receive it. This lack of help perpetuates a vicious cycle—generation after generation of dysfunctional, broken people. God loves these people; He wants to heal them, to deliver them from despair, and to set them free to be the people He created them to be. God made the world and everything in it. He loves His creation; He loves His people. He wants to redeem them from sin and to profoundly change their lives for the better.

Without getting much-needed help, the downward spiral of dysfunctional, self-defeating behavior results in curbing black social and economic progress. On December 28, 2008, Rev. E. Dewey

---

[1]Cornel West, *Hope on a Tightrope: Words and Wisdom* (Carlsbad, CA: Hay House, 2008), 197.
[2]Bill Cosby and Alvin F. Poussaint, *Come On People: On the Path from Victims to Victors* (Nashville: Thomas Nelson, 2007).

Smith, pastor of Greater Traveler's Rest Missionary Baptist Church in Decatur, Georgia, delivered a powerful sermon from Mark 5. He encouraged God's people to be honest about the inner issues that inhibit them from fully experiencing all the good things that God wants for His people. The unclean spirits (v. 2) plaguing lives in the black community can be purged only if people are willing to be honest about them, submit to God's liberation, and follow God's call for a healed and redeemed people to ally themselves with Him in bringing this world into harmony with His will.

In this chapter I will illustrate God's program for dealing with the complex issues raised by Cosby and Poussaint using the context of Isaiah 61. God's way of healing is holistic and is not an end to itself. Confessing to control by unclean spirits, opening up to God's healing, and submitting to a new life calling are fundamental steps in accepting God's gift of grace and redemption for His creation.

> The Spirit of the Lord GOD is upon me,
>   because the LORD has anointed me
> to bring good news to the poor;
>   he has sent me to bind up the brokenhearted,
> to proclaim liberty to the captives,
>   and the opening of the prison to those who are bound;
> to proclaim the year of the LORD's favor,
>   and the day of vengeance of our God;
>   to comfort all who mourn;
> to grant to those who mourn in Zion—
>   to give them a beautiful headdress instead of ashes,
> the oil of gladness instead of mourning,
>   the garment of praise instead of a faint spirit;
> that they may be called oaks of righteousness,
>   the planting of the LORD, that he may be glorified.
> They shall build up the ancient ruins;
>   they shall raise up the former devastations;
> they shall repair the ruined cities,
>   the devastations of many generations. (Isaiah 61:1–4)

LET'S GET REAL

The prophet Isaiah speaks plainly when speaking to Israel about the reality of their situation. Isaiah addresses a people who were enslaved, abused, rejected, ridiculed, segregated, and deeply broken. The terms "poor," "brokenhearted," "captives," "bound," "mourn," "ashes," "a faint spirit," and so on all convey the reality that every life has been devastated and affected by the fall. It is impossible for anyone to live without experiencing struggles, sin, pain, and spiritual death. Everyone suffers because we live in a world ruled by "the prince of the power of the air" (Ephesians 2:2). The world as it exists is not as it should be. We were born into a world at war. The Enemy, the Devil, is real and has wreaked havoc on people's lives for centuries. To deny, minimize, or ignore the Devil's existence leads to self-deception and the acceptance of sinful, self destructive behavior. The horrible pathologies mentioned in the Cosby/Poussaint book reveal the effects of the fall: the black male crisis, out-of-wedlock births, the breakdown of the family and community, bad parenting, substandard education, media consumption without discernment, poor health choices, violence, and poverty. At their roots these are all moral issues, improved only by the actions of a group radicalized for change by beginning the journey of healing.

Illustration #1— Wounded Black Men

Many black men suffer from the dual-edged sword of being over-mothered and under-fathered. God fashioned a child's heart to be radically shaped by the efforts of both parents. Because this is true, poor parenting also contributes to a child's dysfunction. Growing up fatherless may negatively affect developing black males in numerous ways, as Cosby and Poussaint describe in their book. Fatherless boys never learn about fathering and sadly misunderstand the nature of the vocation. Bell Hooks says, "When all black males learn that fatherhood is less about biological creation than about the capacity to nurture the spiritual and emotional growth of a child's life, then they will teach that lesson to the males who come after them."[3] With the absence of many fathers, the lion's share of spiritual and emotional nurturing falls heavily on the shoulders of mothers and grandmothers. As a result, today most black American males grow up in a matriarchy.

In the absence of consistent fathering, most black males are raised in a world dominated by women. Boys socialized by mama and grandmama through their teen years and early adulthood are often unwittingly emasculated. Black sons often become surrogate emotional husbands or surrogate scapegoats for women who are not being loved well by a strong man. Single mothers then use their sons to meet their emotional needs or as objects of their angry frustration. bell hooks describes the psychological scars of over-mothering, which requires black males to surrender their childhoods to satisfy their mothers' unmet emotional needs, this way:

> Dysfunctional single mothers and abused married women who have intense rage toward men who have abandoned them often use male children to meet their emotional needs; this is emotional sexual abuse. In some cases, the mother may be lavishing affection on her son while also being verbally abusive about adult black males. She may say, "all men are dogs," that they are no "good," or that their penises should be "cut off." This teaches the boy fear and mistrust of adult men. It makes him fear becoming an adult man and as a consequence he may try to emotionally remain a boy forever.[4]

hooks highlights the long-term and cyclical consequences of people not getting the help they require. The brokenness of emotionally unhealthy mothers negatively affects their sons. Even worse, over-mothering can also turn sons into future misogynists. Boys raised in a matriarchy often grow to resent the constant control of women. At some point in a boy's journey to manhood, he must break free from the world of women and enter into the world of men. When this occurs, some young men may seek to reassert

[3]bell hooks, *We Real Cool: Black Men and Masculinity* (New York: Routledge, 2004), 107–8.
[4]Ibid., 117.

their masculine identity by taking out their being over-mothered on female peers. This may explain, in part, why some of the worst misogynistic hip-hop music comes out of matriarchal contexts. Many young men retaliate from over-mothering by reasserting dominance over female peers sexually or through physical violence.

Illustration #2—Wounded Black Women

The effects of the fall and the fact of brokenness make life hard for women as well. The absence of good fathers profoundly affects the way in which black women understand their feminine identity. As mentioned earlier, fathers and mothers both play a significant role in the formation of their children. If one of these parental influences is missing, greater opportunity for dysfunction exists. Many black women suffer years of sexual violence at the hands of evil fathers, brothers, cousins, uncles, a mother's boyfriends, neighbors, strangers, and so on. Also many black women shoulder the responsibility of being both father and mother to their children. Black women currently sustain the black church. Many divorced and single moms feel pressured to provide income for themselves and their children with little to no help from the fathers. The many, many demands made on black women create overwhelming stress at times.

In fatherless homes, women's growing up without fathers often creates deep questions about their level of desirability. One of the powerful gifts that fathers give to their daughters is the confidence to know that they are beautiful image bearers of God; they are worth spending time with, listening to, and investing in. Women also want to know, does my father delight in me? When that question remains unanswered because of passive or absent fathers, or is answered no by violent and abusive fathers, young girls often trade their own dignity by substituting unhealthy relationships with male peers. It is no coincidence that the most sexually active girls are those from homes with absent or abusive fathers. Longing for affirmation, girls attempt to answer the question given above by giving their bodies to males who do not love them and have not committed their lives to them publicly. Alternatively, many black women self-medicate the effects of abuse or loneliness by overeating. Obesity among black women sometimes signals women in distress.

The domino effect of brokenness cannot be overstated: broken men vent their brokenness on women and children; broken women vent their brokenness on men and children. Generations of unhealed sin and brokenness produce generations of dysfunctional people. This cycle has destroyed families and communities for years. Brokenness gives birth to more brokenness, and the cycles of dysfunction continue for future generations. Hurting people hurt others.

THE JOURNEY OF HEALING

The good news is that God provides hope for wounded, broken men and women. Isaiah 61 provides hope for God's people by reminding them that God wants to "bind up," "proclaim liberty," "open the prison," "proclaim favor," "comfort" all those who mourn and suffer, and clothe them with new garments. We see here a new identity (a new name), a new hope, and an invitation to enter into healing. God calls His wounded and broken people toward restoration and healing. God has always wanted His people to be free from lives defined by the reality of their sin and brokenness. Healing wounds and restoring humanity are conditions for becoming the kind of people God created before the effects of the fall.

This explains why the good news is so good. This may explain, in part, why Jesus quoted this passage as he inaugurated his public ministry (Luke 4:16–19). Moving toward what God desires for human life involves a necessary process of restoration and healing. The redemption achieved by Jesus Christ is holistic in the sense that it restores the whole creation—especially broken people. Like those in the time of Isaiah, we regularly look for ways to heal our sin, pain, and brokenness artificially. But long-standing coping methods, using artificial and temporary ways of healing and restoration, do not work. They do not deliver because they cannot fill the deep spiritual void that only the triune God can fill.

High school and college boys who habitually smoke pot, for example, often have poor relationships with their fathers. A phrase used in counseling is *acting out*. Acting out involves self-destructive, self-sabotaging behavior in response to negative or harmful experiences. What many fail to see in the social pathologies that plague many black communities is that self-destructive behavior or activities are not always rebellious or defiant but may simply be ways of coping with real pain by acting out, by self-medicating.

Young women act out in response to broken relationships with their fathers by seeking multiple sex partners. Boys acting out because of fatherlessness respond with violence or try to soothe their pain with drugs and alcohol. Many adult women self-medicate their pain by overeating. Many young women lacking consistent love will have a child in order to have someone who finally loves them unconditionally. Men sexually manipulate women to retaliate against matriarchal dominance. Many men try to escape from hopelessness by losing themselves in hours and hours of video games. These are all ways to self-medicate pain. But these methods inevitably do not work. These temporary Band-Aids do not heal the pain, and until people realize this, men and women will never enter the way of freedom and wholeness.

While Cosby and Poussaint make valid points regarding social pathologies, a way to gain and sustain emotional, psychological, and spiritual health is still necessary. The healing to revolutionize the black community in order to experience change must come from transformed hearts and minds.

What Doesn't Work

When confronted with the reality of a fallen, imperfect world, people often seek quick fixes. If they just do this or that and plug into some magic formula, everything will be OK and life will make sense again. Paul Tripp and Tim Lane write about some of the traps people fall into as they wrestle with the harshness of reality.[5]

---

[5]This list originally appeared on the *World Magazine* website, "Time for Change? Now What?" December 9, 2009.

In their book *How People Change*, Timothy Lane and Paul Tripp summarize the false ways people seek change, methods incapable of delivering the internal heart-oriented change really needed. Paraphrased, Lane and Tripp offer the following wisdom:[6]

- *Formalism:* The formalist changes by being a more dutiful Christian. "If I only get more involved in church life, that would grow my faith and make things right again." This person attends church multiple times a week. For him the gospel boils down to participating in the meetings and ministries of the church.
- *Legalism:* The legalist's life centers on a list of do's and don'ts. A legalist's children suffer under the tyranny of performance-oriented conditional love. Being "good" is the goal of the legalist.
- *Mysticism:* The mystic becomes a Christian conference junkie longing for the emotional high of the experience of getting closer to God. Following Christ becomes more about emotional experiences than about transforming into a different kind of person. But the emotional quick fix does not last.
- *Activism:* The activist tries to become closer to God and make sense of life by protesting against "liberals" and other non-conservatives. This person falsely believes that religious consistency equals conservative politics and confuses fighting the culture war with healthy spirituality.
- *Biblicism:* The biblicist, or armchair theologian, fills the gap by learning more information about theology and the Bible. Quick to quote dead theologians and to make a sport of arguing theological minutiae, the biblicist believes that the gospel equals a mastery of biblical content and theology.
- *Psychology-ism:* These people surround themselves with others willing to comfort and pity them for their messed-up lives. The idea is, "I'll get better if the right people support me and listen to my problems." The church means nothing more than a place to heal brokenness. The right support network will change everything. The gospel simply means healing brokenness.
- *Social-ism:* For some people the gospel simply reduces to a network of fulfilling social relationships. These people may belong

---

[6]Ibid.

to two or three different small groups or constantly need to be with other Christians.

• As Lane and Tripp explain, a person like this makes fellowship, acceptance, respect, and position in the body of Christ a replacement for communion with Christ.

What is most compelling about this list is that these things can be both right and wrong. Political activism, biblical knowledge, having good friends, etc. do not address the deep needs that only the work of the Holy Spirit can address: to form and shape us according to the reality of the implications of Jesus's death and resurrection. These temporary balms may seem to fill the void, but they can never deliver what they promise. What really creates change is radical reorientation around the truth of redemption.

What Works

In the book *Broken-Down House*, Paul Trip broadly explains moving forward on the journey toward being a liberated people, free to be fully human through a union with Christ.[7]

First, remember that the fallen world wallows in sinful chaos. It is a mess. Television newscasts air stories about war, famine, disasters, unemployment, the disintegration of families, and personal tragedies—all proof of a fallen creation. The Bible's story reminds believers of the fall, that the Devil successfully tempted Adam and Eve, resulting in an imperfect, sinful world. The good news? That is not the end of the story. God did not abandon His world to chaos. The solution? God plans to redeem and restore all things (Colossians 1; Romans 8) to their intended purpose, so that all spheres of life will reflect His goodness, His grace, and His love. His restored creation will be one in which His people flourish. The flawed, fallen world today offers a distorted, dark view of life; it is all too easy to forget that this world is not the world that is to come, what God intends for His people. Paul Tripp calls this "location amnesia."[8] "Context is your friend," as one professor used to say.

[7]Paul Tripp, *Broken-Down House* (Wapwallopen, PA: Shepherds Press, 2009), 23–86.
[8]Ibid., 25.

The Bible, however, is honest about the world in its fallen state. As Tripp comments, "The history of your Bible drips with the blood of violence, smells of the stench of human greed, betrayal, and perversion. It is stained with instance after instance of people on the one hand forgetting God, while on the other hand doing their best to take his place. Apart from Christ, none of the people in these stories are moral heroes who always get it right."[9] They did not get it right then, and no one gets it right today. Everyone is in the same boat.

Second, understand what *humanity* means. It is primarily important to remember that God created human beings in His likeness and image (Genesis 1:26–28). God gave each human being an identity, a meaning, and a purpose. This view gives each life dignity and worth. God made human beings significantly different from animals, and therefore God gave man responsible dominion over the lower creatures. Human beings must wisely use everything in God's creation for the glory of God and to benefit the world, the community, and the family. Man and woman are part of creation and are thus directly involved in its continuous existence, development, and beautification.

Nonna Verna Harrison neatly summarizes a Christian's worldview in which freedom and responsibility, spiritual perception and relationship with God and neighbor, excellence of character and holiness, royal dignity, priesthood in the created world, and creativity, rationality, the arts, and culture are all elements of what it means to be made in God's image.[10] As such, human beings may freely make decisions in cooperation and in harmony with God. God created humankind to be in union and community with the holy Trinity—the Father, Son, and Holy Spirit. Spiritually, God created humankind for the lifelong process of transformation in order to know and love God and neighbor. This transformation rightly orders our passions, impulses, and reason to excel in moral character and to be freely obedient to the will of God. He endows

---

[9]Ibid., 29.
[10]Nonna Verna Harrison, "The Human Person as Image and Likeness of God," in *The Cambridge Companion to Orthodox Christian Theology*, ed. Mary B. Cunningham and Elizabeth Theokritoff (Cambridge: Cambridge University Press, 2008), 78–90.

all men and women with royal dignity as bearers of His image. They must use their royal status to rule over and simultaneously develop creation.[11] Human beings have a priestly function in the created world. Christ calls them to cosmic priesthood, and this task entails offering the world to God and bestowing God's blessings on the world.[12] Finally, the divine image includes practical reason, which enables all women and men to develop creativity, the arts and sciences, economics, politics, business, and culture.

Third, every man and woman is a sinner. The broken state of the world creates the pain that human beings experience because of the sinful actions of others and because of the broken and sinful responses to those actions. Sin and pain beget more sin and pain. Sadly, the cycle repeats itself in all human communities, neighborhoods, and families. Sin begets sin, but that does not excuse Christians from living responsibly or excuse living in ways contrary to being image bearers of God. God calls Christians to something greater. Again Tripp reminds us that "the biblical doctrine of sin confronts each of us with the reality that we are not as good as we imagine we are, and therefore more needy and vulnerable than we typically consider ourselves to be."[13]

Fourth, Christians must know to whom they belong. As followers of Christ, their union with Christ means so much more than they may realize. God's grace works powerfully in each life to show the desperate need for Jesus, His healing, and His restoration. Understanding that God provides a plan for every Christian offers new hope and potential for amazing change and growth. Forgiveness, deliverance, and enablement play key roles in this spiritual transformation.

The grace of forgiveness means forgiving those who inflicted the wounds of abuse, neglect, omission, and absence. Some wounds result from misdirected good intentions that missed the mark. Returning evil for evil out of defensiveness, self-preservation, and/or

---

[11]Gerard Van Groningen, *From Creation to Consummation*, Vol. I (Dordt, IA: Dordt College Press, 1996), 64–65.
[12]Harrison, "The Human Person as Image and Likeness of God," 86.
[13]Tripp, *Broken-Down House*, 35.

revenge, however, accomplishes nothing but the creation of more sin and pain. Forgiveness is the beginning of liberation from the prison of living in pain. Forgiving is one of the hardest actions a Christian will ever take. True forgiveness does not mean forgetting or ignoring a sin against oneself; rather, the Christian no longer holds the wrong against the sinner in ways that block his ability to love that sinner. In this way a believer lives the gospel and treats others in the very same way God treats His people. The true believer walks the walk instead of just talking the talk.

The grace of deliverance is the recognition that God "got us through" and intends on bringing us into the blessed joys of uniting with the Trinity. Paul Tripp says that we are "loved by a dissatisfied redeemer."[14] Jesus is determined to protect each believer from the enemy and to transform believers into his image. Through the direct work of the Holy Spirit, God wages war against sin, the flesh, and the Devil on the Christian's behalf. Much work must be done in order for the Christian to join God and be with Him in glory.

The grace of enablement means that God's Spirit works in every life to empower His followers to become free and to live as free followers of Christ. God and God alone is the source of power that can unite believers to His Son, deliver them from the power of the Evil One, and set them free to be the people He created them to be in Christ. God enables His people to think, act, feel, emote, and live in new and radical ways. The enabling work of the Spirit that "got us over" in the first place is the same grace that actively works to sustain His healing and redemptive work in each life.

HEALED FOR MISSION

Verse 4 of Isaiah 61 depicts the thrilling vision of a broken and weary people pressed by God to be honest about their sin and devastation. Isaiah prophesies the time when God will transform the downtrodden. God will "build up," "raise up," and "repair" His people. These active verbs illustrate how God's liberating act

---

[14]Ibid., 46.

of personal redemption changes individuals and consequently communities. Salvation spills over and affects the world. God uses His people to bless the nations and to serve as redemptive agents. The context of this purpose, identity, and mission are the ruined and devastated spaces in which God's people find themselves joyfully living. Christ presses His claims and the priorities of the kingdom upon these places.

Living in harmony with God as He changes and conforms His believers from the inside out lends a new perspective on family and community. As Cosby and Poussaint point out, the devastated places in the black community include the black male crisis, the social pathologies of low income neighborhoods, the education and moral crisis among black children, media that promote self-gratification, health-care problems related to bad habits, drug abuse, violence, a discriminatory criminal justice system, and the lack of economic freedom due to opportunity voids and poor financial management.[15]

Union with Christ means relying on His power and His power alone to live in harmony with God's mission for restoration and reconciliation, to do all things for the glory of God and the flourishing of His creation. However, before beginning the journey of healing, it is important to understand why biblical writers do not limit salvation to the realm of personal issues and problems. God helps His people so that they may help others. God uses the redeemed to redeem others. Christians make Christ known to the world by the way they live in their own houses and communities. We need to understand, then, what God's mission is about, what it means to be in the kingdom, and how the grace given to God's people through the work of the Father, Son, and Holy Spirit empowers Christians to be a blessing to their families and neighbors.

An intimate relationship with God the Father, Son, and Holy Spirit demands that Christians orient themselves to certain facts.[16]

---

[15]Cosby and Poussaint, *Come On People*.
[16]Christopher Wright, *The Mission of God: Unlocking the Bible's Grand Narrative* (Downers Grove, IL: InterVarsity Press, 2006), 61–67.

First, Christians worship a God with a mission. The God revealed in the Scriptures is personal, purposeful, and goal-oriented. He created everything for a reason. God's perfect creation then fell because of original sin, the disobedience of Adam and Eve. The Bible's narrative tells the story of God's redemptive purposes unfolding throughout human history, culminating with the eschatological hope of a new creation. Second, if God the Creator has a mission and He created human beings in His image, by definition humankind has a divine calling, a mandate to be fruitful and multiply, to rule, subdue, and cultivate creation. To be human is to have a purposeful role in God's creation. Third, God's people have a specific redemption mission in the history of God's redeeming all things. Since Genesis 12 God has entrusted His people with the mission to be a blessing to the nations for His sake. God charges His people to move into society's devastated, ruined, and broken spaces for the sake of being blessings in ways that only God will make clear. The mission of God's people to "go" make disciples (Matthew 28:19), to go and be witnesses (Acts 1:8) means that God's people are to be committed to participating in God's redemption of the whole creation. Finally, Jesus, the reigning descendant of Jesse and King David, has a mission. The birth, death, and resurrection of Christ fulfill God's promise to His people. The mission of the Davidic heir is both to rule over God's redeemed people and to receive the nations at the ends of the earth as his heritage (Psalm 2:8).

Focusing on the "now what" in the black community touches upon just one aspect of God's redemptive purpose. Being a Christian means that one examines his own holiness in response to God's grace in his personal life, but the Christian also looks at his community in light of (1) God's purpose for His creation, including the redemption of humanity and the creation of the new heavens and new earth; (2) God's purpose for human life in general and all that the Bible teaches about human culture, relationships, ethics, and behavior; (3) God's historical election of His people, their identity and role in relationship to the nations, and the demands He makes about their worship, social ethics, and total value system; (4) the centrality of Jesus of Nazareth, His messianic identity and mission in relationship to Israel and the nations, His cross and resurrection; and finally (5) God's calling of the church, the community of believing Jews and Gentiles who constitute the extended people of the Abrahamic covenant, to be the agent of God's blessing to the nations in the name of the glory of the Lord Jesus Christ.[17]

The Need for a Kingdom Perspective[18]

Jesus invites us to repent because the kingdom is at hand. He invites Christians to look in the mirror, look at their families, neighborhoods, nations, and the world, and recognize that they live for a greater purpose. In order to heal the black community from the pathologies discussed earlier, understanding and applying a contemporary application of Isaiah's teachings requires that Christians work together for the mission of the kingdom.

Jesus emphasized the kingdom of God in His teachings, and by extension so did the apostles. Theological liberalism has emphasized the kingdom while leaving behind Jesus's mission and call to obedience and discipleship. Many evangelicals, while having great passion for the church and mission, often forsake the forest for the trees. They lose the full impact of the gospel on their local culture. A mission-centered worldview orients all of one's life toward the kingdom (Matthew 6:33) and ignites Jesus's followers into radical living here and now.

The kingdom implies more than the salvation of individuals or the reign of God in people's hearts. It means nothing less than the reign of God over his entire created universe. Colossians 1:9–23 reminds us that Jesus as Lord rescues people from darkness, brings them into the kingdom (v. 13), confirms His lordship over all creation (vv. 15–17), establishes His role as sole head of the Church (v. 18), announces His work to reconcile all things in heaven and

[17]Ibid., 67–68.
[18]A version of this section was first published on the Resurgence website (http://theresurgence.com/).

earth (v. 20), and pronounces victory for His people in the great battle between the kingdom of darkness and the kingdom of God's Son (vv. 21–23) (first announced in Genesis 3:15).

The biblical story describes signs of Christ's kingdom: the casting out of demons (Matthew 12:28), the fall of Satan (Luke 10:18), the performance of miracles (Matthew 11:4–5), the preaching of the gospel (Luke 9:6; Romans 16:25), and the forgiveness of sins directly by God in the flesh (Isaiah 33:24; Mark 2:10).

Embracing a kingdom-oriented worldview is also a call to a Spirit-filled mission, orienting all of one's life toward Jesus the King and the Father's purposes for the world. God's people, sent out from the church, bring the kingdom of Jesus to all areas of life mired in sin and brokenness. Jesus's followers act as agents of redemption and restoration for the world (Isaiah 61:1–4). They show the world what it means to live a life reflecting the glory of God in all things: repentance and faith, arts and media, business, education, social life, marriage and family, social justice, caring for the environment, and so on. Being confronted with the kingdom responsibilities of being real, healed, and liberated to be what God has destined one to be in Christ will drive Christians to seek God the Father, Son, and Holy Spirit.

CONCLUSION: THE NEED FOR EMPOWERING GRACE

The same grace that saves and heals us in the name of the Father, the Son, and the Holy Spirit is the same power needed to live kingdom lives in harmony with God's mission. We never stop needing the Holy Spirit. When confronted with the reality of sin and brokenness and a Christian's role in God's plan to restore creation, a Christian's level of spirituality must increase for the following reasons: (1) Christians need a more realistic assessment of who they are in relation to God's mission so that they understand their need of Him. (2) Not surprisingly, they will wish they had more power to change things for the good. Having a kingdom perspective reminds them that they seek God's will on earth as it is in heaven. (3) The craziness of life will tempt Christians to believe that God is not in control of all things. (4) Christians sometimes fear other people instead of waiting for God. At times Christians live in fear instead of trusting in God's sovereign care. (5) A kingdom worldview helps one trust God's wisdom and love without question even in the most horrible times. God is working out His plan in His time. God tests and disciplines those He loves in order to build faith and make His people stronger. Just as a loving father disciplines his children, so God disciplines His people. (6) Trusting God means that one may not understand all that He is doing in the world. Following Jesus requires blind faith at times, without much clarity or explanation. This is Job's story. (7) Christians sometimes look at other people with greater blessings and seemingly easier lives and feel envious; they misunderstand that God acts in each individual's life according to His plan for the kingdom. God's providence works in mysterious ways; the Christian must learn to put his faith in the Lord and not in himself or in other people.

As mentioned earlier, a kingdom-oriented vision for healing means that one cannot be passive.[19] If Christians are to be rebuilders of broken places, they cannot idly sit back and let their families or neighborhoods fall into ruin. The Lord desires that Christians become agents of change. Through the power of the Holy Spirit, Christians can become blessings in their families, communities, and the world. God uses His people to make the world the kind of place that functions in harmony with Him. This sums up the reason for healing and deliverance: to do the good works that God predestined for each of His people in order for them to live for the kingdom and carry out God's plan to redeem the world.

In the end, the type of help, healing, and mission that Isaiah describes explains the importance of the household of faith. God has chosen to bring about great things for the world through God's people in their mutual union in Christ, working out of the mission and calling of the church. The black community needs to recover a sense of the church's mission to follow Christ in bringing about the

---

[19]Tripp, *Broken-Down House*, 137.

redemption of the whole world—people, places, and things. Getting real, getting healed, and being set free is what the church is uniquely equipped to accomplish. Community is vitally important to safely having a context for being honest before God and others about our sin and brokenness (James 5:13–16), for rightly understanding our purpose in living (encouraging each other daily), and for living as persons of blessing to those around us for the mission and glory of God. The key to healing and liberating the black community is in need of revival.

For what does it profit a man to gain the whole world and forfeit his soul?

8

THE BLACK CHURCH AND ORTHODOXY

Anthony Carter

What is orthodoxy? The English word *orthodoxy* comes from the Greek word *orthodoxia*. It is a combination of the words *orthos*, which means "right," and *doxa*, which means "opinion." Orthodoxy, therefore, means having the right opinion or right belief. Christian orthodoxy involves holding to and affirming the right beliefs concerning historical and biblical Christianity, as well as the major doctrines that define what Christianity is and thus distinguishes it from all other religions of the world. Every religion has its standard of orthodoxy; in this respect, Christianity is no different.[1]

Christian orthodoxy has always been understood as being rooted in the Bible as the inspired Word of God. Yet, while the Bible is the place of revealed orthodoxy, the church of Jesus Christ has been the guardian and defender of Christian orthodoxy. Therefore, when the church loses its way and begins to establish orthodoxy apart from the Bible, the church has abdicated its God-ordained calling and its uniqueness in the world. Then rather than being an institution of orthodoxy it becomes duplicitous in the reign of heresy or heterodoxy.[2]

---

[1]According to J. I. Packer, orthodoxy is an idea "rooted in the NT insistence that the gospel has a specific factual and theological content (1 Cor. 15:1–11; Gal. 1:6–9; 1 Tim. 6:3; II Tim. 4:3–4; etc.), and that no fellowship exists between those who accept the apostolic standard of Christological teaching and those who deny it (1 John 4:1–3; II John 7–11)." In *Evangelical Dictionary of Theology*, ed. Walter A. Elwell (Grand Rapids, MI: Baker Books, 1994), 808.

[2]Heterodoxy is an opinion or doctrine, or a system of doctrines, contrary to some established standard of faith such as the Scriptures, the creed or standards of a church, etc.; s.v. *heresy*, http://dictionary.reference.com/browse/heterodoxy.

In *Come On People* Bill Cosby and Alvin Poussaint call African-Americans to a kind of social and communal orthodoxy. They have called for a right opinion or belief about ourselves that will lead to a right demonstration of constructive, and not destructive, behavior. This orthodoxy is based upon the universal principles of love, respect, hope, and caring and comprehends a concern for the overall welfare of the community. Their desire is for a community of people who realize that caring for and respecting each other begins with caring for and respecting oneself. However, though it begins there, according to Cosby and Poussaint it does not stop there. It must reach its fulfillment in realizing that the health of one is achieved for the benefit and the health of all. Nevertheless, articulating and guarding orthodoxy typically has been the realm of the church. Thus, even in espousing their views of African-American society and offering corrections and solutions, Cosby and Poussaint frequently refer to the church.

Cosby and Poussaint do not have a chapter dedicated to the church and its role in a virtuous society. However, throughout the book it is clear that they envision a community where the places of worship, particularly churches, play a significant role in the articulation, demonstration, and reinforcement of the values Cosby and Poussaint espouse. According to Cosby and Poussaint:

> The black church has always been a force for black people throughout the worst times in our history. The church is a key player in the black extended family. We would not have much of a village if we didn't have the church and other faith-based organizations.[3]

They speak of the church as a civic organization—an institution whose primary role is social reform, thus praising the church for its utilitarian purposes. The church is useful in fostering a society where social ills are alleviated. Consequently, the church is called

---

[3]Bill Cosby and Alvin F. Poussaint, *Come On People: On the Path from Victims to Victors* (Nashville: Thomas Nelson, 2007), 43.

on by Cosby and Poussaint to get more active in addressing issues of mental health,[4] sexual promiscuity and disease (including the promotion of condom use),[5] producing healthy food alternatives,[6] speaking out against self-degrading music,[7] promoting and pulling together the family,[8] calling deadbeat dads to assume their responsibilities,[9] and many other socially responsible agendas.

No one argues about the church being called to be an institution of change for our society. Taking up the cause of social injustice and seeking to bring health, education, respect, and responsibility to the world is well within the realm and calling of the church in the world. Nevertheless, while it is *a* calling, it is not *the* calling.

THE CALL OF THE CHURCH

Acts 3:1–7 records the account of the apostles Peter and John being confronted by a lame man begging outside the temple. He accosted the apostles and asked them for help. Peter looked at the man with compassion and said, "I have no silver and gold, but what I do have I give to you. In the name of Jesus Christ of Nazareth, rise up and walk!"

Today the church in America can no longer say, "We have no silver and gold." The coffers of the church are filled. Megachurches abound. High-priced evangelists and self-proclaimed prophets fly across the country (some in private jets) selling their latest schemes of health, wealth, and prosperity. American Christianity is awash in consumerism, and the African-American church is the most prolific of the consumers.[10] Indeed, the church can no longer say it does not have silver and gold. Unfortunately, neither can it say, "but what I do have I give to you."

---

[4]Ibid., 186.
[5]Ibid., 180.
[6]Ibid., 172.
[7]Ibid., 145.
[8]Ibid., 83–84.
[9]Ibid., 143.
[10]According to researchers George Barna and Harry Jackson Jr., "there is a higher percentage of large black congregations than there is among white or Hispanic congregations. In fact, while Willow Creek and Saddleback are regularly touted by the media as the biggest churches in North America, there are at least a dozen black churches whose attendance exceeds either of those well known congregations by at least a couple thousand people per week!" George Barna and Harry Jackson Jr., *High Impact African-American Churches* (Ventura, CA: Regal Books, 2004), 28.

What was once the treasure chest of the church—namely, the person of Christ and the message of the gospel—has been exchanged for social expediency and financial gain. What has been lost, indeed forfeited, is an uncompromised, orthodox, biblical view of Jesus and the message of the gospel that saves sinners from the death that is due to all of us because of our sin. What has been lost is the unique message and calling of the church.

Contrary to popular notions and suggestions, even by Cosby and Poussaint, the primary purpose of the church is not the healing of social ills or the righting of social injustices. The church was not given the treasure chest that is the gospel of Jesus Christ for the purpose of clothing the naked, feeding the hungry, or demonstrating against abortion. All such issues are important, and the church should seek to address them in their proper context, but not at the expense of its primary objective and calling—namely, the saving of souls through the proclamation of the gospel.

No other institution has been entrusted with so important—even eternally consequential—a message as the church has been. No other institution has been given the invaluable treasure that is the promise of the forgiveness of sins and eternal life through Jesus Christ. When we forfeit this most precious treasure for political expediency, financial gain, or social reform, we not only surrender our God-given birthright but also lose any real, unique, lasting (in fact everlasting) help we can offer the world.

The world is filled with institutions ready and able to feed the hungry. The world is overrun with individuals and organizations desiring to heal the sick and to bring justice to the disenfranchised and education to the illiterate. Yet there is only one place people can go to hear the message of redemption from sin and eternal life in Jesus Christ. That place is the church. When the church forfeits the uniqueness of the gospel and turns it into a social construction for social empowerment and political change, it ceases to be the eternal change agent for which Christ gave his life.

Yes, the church is called to engage in the social well-being of society. Every church needs to be doing all it can to minister to the needs of its community. However, it must do so with the understanding that the need that most uniquely relates to the calling of the church is the salvation of souls from a far worse condition than poverty, hunger, or disease. The church is called to preach salvation from sin and death through Jesus Christ alone. This is her orthodoxy.

Jesus Himself asked the all-important, immediately relevant, rhetorical question, "For what does it profit a man to gain the whole world and forfeit his soul?" (Mark 8:36). The obvious answer is, "nothing." Orthodoxy serves as a reminder of the mission and message of the church. The mission is the worship of God through Jesus Christ. The message is repentance from sin and faith in Jesus Christ for the redemption of body and soul from hell and unto eternal life. The church is the only place where eternal profits are guaranteed to all who place their faith in Jesus Christ. There are infinite ways to lose your soul. There is only one way to save it. The church has the way. It must reclaim it. This is the heart of orthodoxy.

RECOVERING A BIBLICAL ORTHODOXY

What do you believe? Now there is a question that has fallen out of favor in our modern parlance. In our days of subjectivity and the reign of narcissism, the objectivity of truth and its inherent transforming quality is woefully neglected, to the detriment of all society. The society that seeks to throw off the constraints of objectivity and by virtue of this casting off declares itself to be free is actually more in bondage than it ever imagined. Jesus declared unequivocally that it is the truth—objective reality—that sets one free.[11] And then He declared Himself to be that truth[12]—the most objective demonstration of reality the world has ever seen. Therefore it is the truth—namely Jesus—that sets men and women free. This freedom gives us a higher purpose for which to live and helps us realize that life is not about us.[13]

---

[11]John 8:32.
[12]John 14:6.
[13]Rick Warren captured this pathos in his best-selling book *The Purpose Driven Life*. He began the book with the now-famous and heart-resonating words, "It's not about you."

On the other hand, the neglecting of truth has led to a plethora of social and emotional woes that have infected American culture in general and African-American culture in particular. It has produced a moral vacuum, the vacuum that Cosby and Poussaint seek to address.

In *Come On People* they attempt to address the moral decline of our society and suggest positive societal moorings as the answer. We must commend Cosby and Poussaint for having the courage to address some of our society's sacred cows (hip-hop music, unhealthy foods, television, etc.) and to suggest that not everything that feels good to us is good for us. They write with a confidence and concern that demands our attention.

However, while seeking to posit objective truth, Cosby and Poussaint failed to establish an identifiable standard for their truth. Bill Cosby is an admired actor and activist, but that does not make him an authority on black culture and society. Alvin Poussaint is a respected psychiatrist, but that does not mean that his opinions on objective standards of morality are true. There must be an objective standard or everything and everyone becomes his or her own standard of truth.

Ironically, Cosby and Poussaint understand this and have sought to speak in terms of objective and absolute values, though not declaring the foundations for such assertions. Perhaps it is understood or assumed. Perhaps they know that there is a long-standing standard of morality that undergirds African-American life. Yet what they assume, I want to declare openly: the only standard to which we can call all people and expect conformity is the standard set by the Creator God. It is the reality of God and the right beliefs and understandings (orthodoxy) that must follow in order to produce right living. Thus orthodoxy begins with the Word of God.

THE BIBLE AS THE SOURCE OF ORTHODOXY

Orthodoxy is based on the Bible as the Word of God. There is a word from God for our times, as there always has been. Orthodox

Christians have always understood this to be true. The Bible has long served as the standard of truth for the African-American church and society. Those who would teach contrary and lead others to do the same will find themselves on the wrong side of God and orthodoxy.

From the beginning of African-American history, this has been the case. Among the first religious writers and Christian preachers of African-American descent there was adherence to the objective standard of the Bible as the Word of God. Jupiter Hammon (1711–1806?), one of the earliest African-American writers, wrote concerning the Bible's authority and standard for living:

> The Bible is the word of God and tells you what you must do to please God. . . . In the Bible, God had told us everything it is necessary we should know in order to be happy here and hereafter. The Bible is a revelation of the mind and will of God to men.[14]

Christian orthodoxy is a matter of biblical record. The black church in America has historically held to orthodoxy. It has done so through a high view of Scripture, believing the Bible to be the inspired Word of God. One contemporary African-American author and historian has made this point:

> Our forefathers understood that the contents of the Scriptures were powerful because they contain the message of God to his people. Reading the Bible was the dying ambition of many slaves. Its words were manna from heaven for a starving soul. *Inerrant* and *inspired* were not common parlance, but the *ideas* these words represent were once commonly held. It was the perspective of our earliest leaders and thinkers.[15]

The African-American church used to be a stronghold for bib-

---

[14]Jupiter Hammon, "Address to the Negroes in the State of New York," in Sondra O'Neale, *Jupiter Hammon and the Biblical Beginnings of African-American Literature* (Metuchen, NJ: The American Theological Library Association and the Scarecrow Press), 237.
[15]Thabiti Anyabwile, *The Decline of African-American Theology* (Downers Grove, IL: Intervarsity Press, 2007), 241, italics in original.

lical orthodoxy.[16] Even during the civil rights era when the black
church was most active in pursuing social reform, the vast majority
of predominantly African-American churches was orthodox. It was
still an institution committed to the message of Jesus Christ and was
resolute in its belief that the Bible is the inspired and infallible source
of that message. Whether the issue was the abolition of slavery or
the end of separate but equal, the black church managed to fulfill its
social responsibility while maintaining the highest view of Scripture
and primary message of salvation. Yet these foundational sentiments and convictions have waned in our day. The tragedy is that
the Bible has lost its preeminent place as the source of orthodoxy
in many black churches, and we seem to no longer believe that it is
sufficient for revealing to us the mind and will of God for our lives
together. One contemporary rap group has well captured the loss of
the supremacy of Scripture in our time:

Sufficiency of scripture
How it used to be a fixture,
Now it's swirled into a world mixture
Expose the fallacy of this mentality
Lord, restore Your word to its centrality![17]

There is a prophetic word! "Lord, restore Your word to its
centrality."

Unfortunately, as the church became more political, it decided
that integrating lunch counters was more important than the integrity of the faith.[18] Don't misunderstand me: I am not arguing for
an either/or understanding of social responsibility and theological
integrity. On the contrary, I would argue for a both/and. The church

---

[16]For a more comprehensive study of the development of early African-American theology and
orthodoxy and the nature of the subsequent and unfortunate decline, see ibid.
[17]Christcentric, "Sufficiency of Scripture," Reformation, 2006.
[18]For all the social good that the nonviolent civil rights movement accomplished, it also initiated the mass decline in historic orthodox biblical convictions within the black church. James R.
Washington commented at the time, "The nonviolent movement has added to the evidence that
Negro houses of worship are essential as meeting places and that black religion is a source of
Negro leadership. But the movement has also declared that every other aspect of Christianity is of
limited value and interest." Joseph R. Washington, Black Religion: The Negro and Christianity in
the United States (Boston: Beacon Press, 1966), 28.

of Jesus Christ has a calling for both theological integrity and social responsibility. However, biblical orthodoxy must have the primacy and must direct and correct all social agendas. Unfortunately, this has not been the norm of late. For the most part the black church has sacrificed her theologically orthodox heritage for political expediency and social reform.[19] And when the church moves away from a biblical, humble, objective orthodoxy, it inevitably replaces it with an unbiblical, human-centered, subjective orthodox, which is no orthodoxy at all. Sadly, such has become the case in the black church in America.

Fortunately, it has not always been the case, and it need not be the case in the future. The call to social reform among black Americans must also be a call to reform among predominantly black churches. This needs to begin with a return to and a reaffirmation of what we believe.

WE BELIEVE . . .

The oldest statement and most commonly held affirmation of orthodoxy may be found in what is known as the Apostles' Creed. This creed is believed to be the earliest ecumenical statement or set of commonly held Christian beliefs. *Creed* comes from the Latin word *credo*, meaning "I believe." It is called *The Apostles'* Creed because, though some have erroneously believed that the apostles originally wrote the statement, it claims to be a biblically consistent summation of what the apostles taught.[20] It was written during the first few centuries of the church, and today it is the most widely held and commonly agreed upon expression of the core doctrines of Christian belief. Therefore, it is safe to say that while not all orthodoxy is contained in the creed, any statement concerning orthodoxy must begin with the Apostles' Creed and the application of it.

The oldest formal African-American denomination is the African Methodist Episcopal Church. Believed to have been founded in

---

[19]Like Esau in the Bible, we have sold our theological birthright for that which is fleeting and only momentary (see Genesis 25:29–34).
[20]*Evangelical Dictionary of Theology*, 72.

1787, it is the longest enduring denomination of predominantly African-American Christians.[21] Today this long-standing church states: "To find the basic foundations of the beliefs of the African Methodist Episcopal Church, you need look no further than The Apostles' Creed. . ." The Creed states:

> I believe in God the Father Almighty, Maker of heaven and earth, and in Jesus Christ his only son our Lord who was conceived by the Holy Spirit, born of the Virgin Mary, suffered under Pontius Pilate, was crucified, dead, and buried. The third day he arose from the dead; he ascended into heaven and sitteth at the right hand of God the Father Almighty; from thence he shall come to judge the quick and the dead. I believe in the Holy Spirit, the Church Universal, the communion of saints, the forgiveness of sins, the resurrection of the body and the life everlasting. Amen.[22]

The creed begins where all orthodoxy must begin and where biblical orthodoxy in our day must be reclaimed—namely, with belief in God.

We Believe in God

It could and should be argued that the creed of African-American culture has always been, "We believe in God." This affirmation has been the least common denominator that has united virtually all African-Americans and has been the rallying point for most of the major advancements in African-American culture.

Atheism, while growing in popularity in European culture, has never been a popular philosophy in America. This is even more acutely accurate among African-Americans. Those who would dare raise the banner of atheism (or even the more skeptical notion of agnosticism) within the African-American community would have very few allies.

Throughout the history of America, the vast majority of those

---

[21]Henry H. Mitchell, *Black Church Beginnings: The Long-Hidden Realities of the First Years* (Grand Rapids, MI: Wm. B. Eerdmans, 2004), 66.
[22]See http://www.ame-church.com/about-us/beliefs.php.

who spoke most eloquently and most powerfully for the cause of African-American hopes and dreams have been men and women of faith. From the illiterate black slave organizers to the first black intellectuals there is a common thread that is woven throughout their tapestry, an understanding that echoes with singular clarity in their voices: "We believe in God Almighty, the Creator of heaven and earth."

From Jupiter Hammon to Phyllis Wheatley, from Nat Turner to Frederick Douglass to Booker T. Washington, from Marcus Garvey to Malcolm X and Martin Luther King Jr.—those who desired to move African-Americans forward have done so understanding that there is a God, an Almighty Creator who is with us and for us. Today is no different. From Russell Simmons and Denzel Washington to Oprah Winfrey and Cornel West to the Congressional Black Caucus and the President of the United States, African-American cultural icons still confess overwhelmingly, "We believe in God." Cosby and Poussaint seem to assume this, but an outright statement of this belief and the necessary accountability inherent in it is foundational to any cultural or moral reformation.

There must be a higher authority, a standard of righteousness to which all men are called if our proposals for change are going to have validity and substance. That authority must rest in a sovereign Creator who holds all people accountable for their actions. A call to morality must always begin with a call to God. The church that recovers this foundational truth and waves the banner of our accountability before God will be a church whose orthodoxy has relevance for our time.

We Believe in Jesus

At the heart of Christian orthodoxy is the person and work of Jesus Christ. No church can be taken seriously and no expression of Christianity can have any validity if it does not affirm the centricity of Christ. Therefore, the Apostles' Creed, while beginning with God the Father, says most when it confesses the truth about Jesus Christ.

No doubt, Jesus Christ is a polarizing figure. He does not suffer fence-sitters[23] or those who see him simply as a good teacher or example and not as Lord.[24] Jesus demands total allegiance.[25] Historically, the Church has affirmed this as well. The church of Jesus Christ has long asserted the uniqueness of Jesus and his lordship. And the church that once unashamedly asserted the uniqueness of Christ needs to do so again. Orthodoxy demands it, and our world needs it.

The church that once declared there is salvation in no other name than Jesus needs to declare it still. The church that once held out faith in Jesus Christ as the only means of redemption from sin and as the only hope for the world must affirm it once again. The world needs the church to be the bastion of orthodoxy it is called to be. The African-American community needs it too. At the heart is the proclamation of the person and work of Jesus.

Some may suggest that the claims of Christ are not relevant for our times. Yet the church must not only insist that Christ is relevant but must demonstrate this as well. Orthodoxy demands that we do so. Understood biblically, the death and resurrection of Christ, taken together as one, is not only the most significant event in history but is at the same time the most relevant. Christ walked out of the grave on the first Easter morning, and so did hope.

It should not surprise us that the first African-American US president was elected on a platform built around the idea of hope. No matter how prosperous or impoverished people believe themselves to be, what keeps us moving is hope. No institution in the history of America has instilled more hope in more people than has the church, and particularly the black church. We are reminded that the song known as the "Negro National Anthem" states, "Sing a song full of the faith that the dark past has taught us, / Sing a song full of the *hope* that the present has brought us."[26] Hope has always been a hallmark of the black church. Why? Why this emphasis and articulation of hope? Because at the heart of the gospel message is

[23]Matthew 10:37–38.
[24]Luke 18:18–30.
[25]John 12:23–26.
[26]James Weldon Johnson, "Lift Every Voice and Sing," 1899, emphasis mine.

the good news that God in Jesus Christ has brought love, light, and hope into the world. And this hope was perfectly displayed in the resurrection of Jesus Christ.

If we have a generation of people who act out hopelessness and self-destructive despair, the answer is the resurrection of Christ. Cosby and Poussaint are correct when they assert that Christianity once offered hope.[27] I assert that when Christianity affirms its God-given orthodoxy it still offers hope—the only real, lasting hope. It is a hope that sin can be forgiven, guilt removed, and shame overcome. The healing of families and communities must begin with the healing of sin-ravished souls. Proclaiming the cross is the business of the church of Christ. Yet, part of the hopelessness that plagues our community is a result of the church's abandoning the message of Christ and trading it for a message of financial prosperity and political influence. It is not surprising that the Bible says that such people are to be most pitied in this world, because they have abandoned the one true source of lasting hope.[28] The only hope for a seemingly hopeless world is the resurrection of Christ. The faithful, orthodox believing church has always affirmed and demonstrated this truth. We must do so once again. It is the greatest gift we can give to a hopeless world.

We Believe in Life after Death

Perhaps nothing has produced more morally devastating effects as has the failure of Americans in general and African-Americans in particular to seriously consider that this life is not the end. Materialism, hedonism, and narcissism have so infected our age that one is hard-pressed to believe that this present generation would have survived a day in the world a hundred or even fifty years ago. Cosby, in his assessment of the moral decay he witnesses, states:

> I have seen enough to know that, no matter what people tell you, this mayhem is not a part of our culture the way our music is. This

---

[27]Cosby and Poussaint, *Come On People*, 33.
[28]1 Corinthians 15:17–19.

violence is not a part of our culture the way our literature is. And this vulgarity has never been a part of our culture before.[29]

The richest, smartest, healthiest generation of African-Americans today is also the spiritually weakest, poorest, and sickest generation this world has ever seen. This is largely due to the shortsightedness that has gripped us. We have lost sight of everything except the immediate—what is immediately available to me and how I might indulge myself today. Someone has said that the creed of our generation is, "Get all you can and can all you get." We desire no satisfaction except that which brings immediate pleasure. Delayed gratification is a cursed idea.

Culpable in this generation's grab for the immediate is the church that has lost its orthodox understanding of heaven and hell and reward and punishment. The emphasis in the most prominent places of worship across the country is rich and lavish lifestyles. It is a focus on getting financial and physical blessings. Today little is spoken concerning the emphasis in the Bible on tomorrow and eternity. Yet Jesus himself declared unambiguously:

> Do not lay up for yourselves treasures on earth, where moth and rust destroy and where thieves break in and steal, but lay up for yourselves treasures in heaven, where neither moth nor rust destroys and where thieves do not break in and steal. For where your treasure is, there your heart will be also.[30]

The lack of orthodoxy has led to a church that seemingly teaches the very opposite of what Jesus taught. Rather than labor for eternity, churchgoers are told to labor for today. In the one place where the world should hear a message of eternity and delayed gratification, it is hearing a message of immediate satisfaction. The church would serve the world well if it proclaimed once again the orthodox understanding of heaven and hell and how an eternal perspective needs to trump a temporal perspective.

[29]Cosby/Poussaint, *Come On People*, xvii.
[30]Matthew 6:19–21.

Jupiter Hammon, writing to his fellow slaves, stated that the most important thing was not that they become free, but that they be saved from their sins and the punishment of eternal death. He wrote:

> But this, my dear brethren, is by no means the greatest thing we have to be concerned about. Getting our liberty in this world is nothing to our having the liberty of the children of God. Now the Bible tells us that we are all, by nature, sinners, that we are slaves to sin and Satan, and that unless we are converted, or born again, we must be miserable forever. Christ says that except a man be born again, he cannot see the kingdom of God and all that do not see the kingdom of God must be in the kingdom of darkness. There are but two places where all go after death, white and black, rich and poor: those places are heaven and hell. Heaven is a place made for those who are born again and who love God, and it is a place where they will be happy forever. Hell is a place made for those who hate God and are his enemies and where they will be miserable for all eternity.[31]

Hammon, like most of the African-American Christians of his day, had his orthodoxy in order. Being free from slavery was a great concern and one for which Hammon and others were ready to give their lives. But Christian slaves understood that freedom from oppression was not as important as was freedom from sin, death, and judgment. This provided motivation for living and hope for tomorrow.

Today we need men and women who will say along with Hammon that immediate goals are worthwhile, but they must not be obtained at all costs. The church needs to be a bastion and beacon of eternity in a world that is consumed with the here and now. Our community desperately needs biblical orthodoxy. The world needs it too.

---

[31]Jupiter Hammon, "An Address to the Negroes," in O'Neale, *Jupiter Hammon and the Biblical Beginnings of African-American Literature*, 236.

ONLY THE CHURCH: RECLAIMING ORTHODOXY

The tragedy of too many predominantly African-American churches is that they have gained much of the world but are losing their souls. Prophetic voices have been sold and silenced for political favors and esteem. For example, a church too closely allied to the Democratic Party in decrying social inequalities and promoting the cause of civil rights can lose its voice in the fight against the slaughter of millions of babies through the ungodly abortion industry. Conversely, a church too closely allied with the Republican Party may find a voice to sound forth the evil of abortion but will find little credibility with those who lack affordable health care and are on the wrong end of economic policies that profit the rich.

The church that has no allegiance except the Lord Jesus Christ and His kingdom can and must speak prophetically and even poetically on the evils of abortion and unjust wars, on the inequitable administration of the death penalty, and on pay inequity suffered by women. The church of Jesus Christ does have social responsibilities. It is responsible for equipping Christians with the message of the gospel so they can go into the world and be agents of hope, change, and eternal life. In doing so, the church produces citizens who are good neighbors and friends.

However, when the church loses its message and mission, so too do individual Christians. The call of Cosby and Poussaint is a call to social reform. Yet, before the church can reform society in a way that honors God, it must first reform itself and reclaim the orthodoxy that gives it power and authority in this world.

How do we accomplish the reclamation of orthodoxy and the centrality of Jesus Christ in the mission and message of the church? Others have written well on this subject.[32] Here I offer a few, though not exhaustive, suggestions:

1. *The church needs to recommit itself to the Bible as the Word of God.* For too long the African-American church has let the media, society, politicians, and even its own members set the agenda. We

---

[32]Anyabwile, *Decline of African-American Theology*, 237–246.

have let self-aggrandizing pastors and bishops decide what is best for the church (and thus themselves) and have in turn not given Scripture its rightful place in the life of the church. Healthy, biblical orthodoxy begins with understanding that the Bible is the Word of God and that it speaks infallibly as it sets the agenda for the church and for individual Christians as well. The Bible makes this claim for itself: "All Scripture is breathed out by God and profitable for teaching, for reproof, for correction, and for training in righteousness, that the man of God may be complete, equipped for every good work" (2 Timothy 3:16–17).

2. *The church needs to recommit itself to the uniqueness of its mission and message.* Only the church of Jesus Christ has the message of Jesus as the hope and Savior of the world. Only the church has a message that will not only benefit humanity in time, but more importantly in eternity. Only the church has the answer for the sin and guilt that plagues individuals and nations. When the church is living out the true calling of its creed—namely, the proclamation of Jesus Christ as Savior and Lord—it is being what God called it to be—namely, a light to the nations. Orthodoxy reclaimed is the best hope the church has of really offering hope to a hopeless world. Our world is no more needful than was the world of Paul's day, and yet Paul declared, "For since, in the wisdom of God, the world did not know God through wisdom, it pleased God through the folly of what we preach to save those who believe. For Jews demand signs and Greeks seek wisdom, but *we preach Christ crucified*, a stumbling block to Jews and folly to Gentiles, but to those who are called, both Jews and Greeks, Christ the power of God and the wisdom of God" (1 Corinthians 1:21–24).

3. *The church needs to once again clarify its doctrinal distinctives.* The life and living of the church is rightly connected to the doctrinal preaching and teaching of the church. A church that is awash in moral failure can too often trace those failures to a decline in the biblical clarity and doctrinal integrity of its teaching and preaching. Unfortunately, it is common today to downplay doctrine

and to stay away from it because "it might divide us." But it is the nature of truth to divide. Orthodoxy by definition is opinionated and, when necessary, dogmatic. A society morally adrift (where right is too frequently called wrong and wrong is all too often called right) does not need a church unsure of what it believes.[33] The church needs to sound a clear call for truth and moral standards. However, without biblical parameters of truth, the standards of right and wrong are not only lost in our churches but also in our homes and community. Therefore, "let us hold fast the confession of our hope without wavering, for he who promised is faithful" (Hebrews 10:23).

4. *The church needs to recover its connection with the history of the Christian church.* Ask the average American churchgoer his understanding of church history, and inevitably he will begin rehearsing the immediate history of the building in which they meet weekly for worship. For most, the history we know is no more than those snippets of information (minus the splits and court battles) that is shared annually during the weeklong church anniversary. While there is a place for this immediate recollection, a more needful understanding is the identification we have with the saints of past ages and cultures. Connecting with the church through the centuries will remind us that we have an orthodoxy that has been claimed and reclaimed throughout the years and has not only informed the church but sustained her in some of her most trying times. It will remind us that we do not need a new orthodoxy, only new voices and new methods of making historical orthodoxy known. Remember the admonition, "Therefore, since we are surrounded by so great a cloud of witnesses, let us also lay aside every weight, and sin which clings so closely, and let us run with endurance the race that is set before us, looking to Jesus, the founder and perfecter of our faith, who for the joy that was set before him endured the cross, despising the shame, and is seated at the right hand of the throne of God" (Hebrews 12:1–2).

Today some are calling for a new theology, while others are

---

[33]Isaiah 5:20.

proclaiming that God is doing a "new thing." On the contrary, we do not need a new theology; we need to recover the orthodoxy that has already been delivered to the church by the Spirit of God.[34] The test of orthodoxy is to place it in differing contexts and not have it change, but rather watch as it changes people. It will produce voices unique to its time, decrying the evils of its day, yet never denouncing or denying the source from which it springs—namely, the Bible, the inspired, all-sufficient Word of God—or the message and mission of that source—namely, Jesus Christ and eternal life through Him.

The world is waiting.

---

[34]Isaiah 5:20; Jude 3.

9

THE PROSPERITY GOSPEL

Ken Jones

Where does one begin when addressing the poisonous strand of American evangelicalism known by such labels as "word of faith," "name it and claim it," or the "prosperity gospel"? So much has transpired since Walter Martin (the original *Bible Answer Man* radio host) called attention to this danger lurking on the sidelines of evangelicalism, both on his radio program and in his classic work *The Kingdom of the Cults*. Martin's successor, Hank Hanegraaff, has continued to carry the torch on the air and with two books of his own, *Christianity in Crisis* and *Counterfeit Revival*. Yet, despite the clarion call of these diligent servants, the prosperity gospel not only flourishes but has become the norm within the rank and file of evangelical Christianity. Let me begin by turning to one of the prosperity gospel proponents for a definition of this school of thought. What follows are statements taken from the Creflo Dollar website:

> Poverty is not the will of God for any believer. . . . From Genesis to Revelation, the Bible proves that poverty goes against everything God desires for believers. Poverty is a spirit designed to keep believers in financial bondage. . . . You were made wealthy and rich before you came into existence. You've been predestined to prosper financially. . . . As the righteousness of God, your inheritance of wealth and riches is included in the "spiritual blessings" (or spiritual things) the Apostle Paul spoke of in Ephesians 1:5. Based on Psalm 112:3 righteousness, wealth and riches go hand in hand. You have every right to possess material wealth, clothes,

jewelry, houses, cars and money in abundance. . . . The Bible says that wealth is stored up for the righteous (Proverbs 13:22, *New American Standard*). However, it will remain stored up until you claim it. Therefore claim it now! You possess the ability to seize and command wealth and riches to come to you (Deuteronomy 8:18). Exercise that power by speaking faith-filled words daily and taking practical steps to eradicate debt. Like God, you can speak spiritual blessings into existence (Romans 4:17). . . . For more information on how to obtain the wealth that has been stored up for you purchase the single message "A Mandate for Prosperity" available now.[1]

But wait, there's more. On the website for World Changers Church International, Dollar's church, two bullet points highlight "The School of Prosperity": "Why God wants you rich" and "How to use biblical principles to make natural principles work on your behalf."[2] Perhaps there was always a time when this emanated from the fringes of evangelicalism. But on any given Sunday many of the above quotations can be heard in varying degrees from numerous evangelical churches that don't espouse the gospel of prosperity. David Van Biema and Jeff Chu illustrate this point in an article posted September 10, 2006, on the *Time* magazine website citing a poll in which 61 percent of Christians surveyed believe that God wants people to be prosperous and 31 percent agreed that if you give your money to God, God will reciprocate.[3]

The prosperity gospel's crossover impact is illustrated by the wildly successful little book *The Prayer of Jabez*, written by Bruce Wilkinson, a respected Bible teacher and founder of Walk Thru the Bible Ministries. *The Prayer of Jabez* spread through the evangelical community like wildfire, not because people were appalled at its content, but because they found the book helpful. The subtitle of the book, "Breaking Through to the Blessed Life," not only indicates the aim of the book but also reflects the evangelical mind-set that

---

[1]See http://www.creflodollarministries.org/BibleStudy/Articles.aspx?id=303.
[2]See http://www.worldchangers.org/soponline/soplanding.html?site=CDM.
[3]David Van Biema and Jeff Chu, "Does God Want You to Be Rich?"; http://www.time.com/time/magazine/article/0,9171,1533448,00.html.

has allowed aberrant "word of faith" teaching to become normative, if not the new orthodoxy. Wilkinson says in his preface:

> Dear Reader,
>   I want to teach you how to pray a daring prayer that God always answers. It is brief, only one sentence with four parts, and tucked away in the Bible, but I believe it contains the key to a life of extraordinary favor with God. This petition has radically changed what I expect from God and what I experience every day by His power. In fact, thousands of believers who are applying its truths are seeing miracles happen on a regular basis.[4]

Two things strike me as I reflect on these words. First, I am struck by how removed this respected Bible teacher is from historic Christian teaching on matters like gaining God's favor. But also I am struck by how much this preface sounds like something straight from a word of faith pulpit. Wilkinson's book was published in 2000; since then prosperity theology has spilled over into the mainstream of American Christianity. I don't know how important it is to question where the teaching originated, although many would posit it began with Pentecostalism. I think the more pressing question is this: how did it find its way into the very heart of orthodox Christian teaching? An early twentieth-century circuit preacher named Samuel Morris angered many churches for interpreting 1 Corinthians 6:19 to mean that an indwelling Holy Spirit imputes human divinity. George Baker, one of Morris's disciples, took this teaching even further, dubbing himself "Father Divine." Father Divine took his show on the road to the backwoods of Georgia in 1912. But his eccentric claims of divinity alienated the very churches providing him a platform. Father Divine was arrested in Valdosta, Georgia, in 1914 as a public nuisance and was considered possibly insane.

Yet few even raise an eyebrow when prosperity preacher Kenneth Copeland claims, "You don't have a God living in you;

---

[4]Bruce Wilkinson, *The Prayer of Jabez* (Sisters, OR: Multnomah, 2000), preface.

you are one. You are part and parcel of God."[5] Copeland, of course, is much celebrated, not ejected from the church. Walter Martin and Hank Hanegraaff saw something terribly wrong with these statements, but many professing Christians don't recognize the harm. Again the question has been raised: how did we come to accept the absurdities of the prosperity gospel? The simple answer reflects a seismic shift in Christian thinking, specifically as it relates to man, God, and the Bible. This non-creedal, non-confessional Christianity raises expectations and assumptions about and from the Christian faith that simply fail theological or historical scrutiny. The prosperity gospel simply mirrors that shift. Notice how Creflo Dollar and Bruce Wilkinson both assume that human success and fulfillment (as defined by them) is what God desires for His people. Furthermore, both are convinced that certain principles in the Bible, when applied and practiced correctly, will bring about God's will of blessings and prosperity. Reformed theologian Michael Horton, a keen observer of this shift in evangelical thought, noted, "A number of theologians have pointed out the striking similarities between this prosperity message and ancient Gnosticism. Like the ancient heresy, the Word of Faith message assumes a sharp dualism between spirit and matter, promising mastery over one's external circumstances by learning the secret principles of the invisible realm."[6]

Two main roads created the intersection and convergence of orthodox teaching and the prosperity movement. On the one hand there is the path blazed by E. W. Kenyon, dubbed by D. R. McConnell as the father of the modern word of faith movement. Kenyon was not a Pentecostal but traveled in Pentecostal circles and greatly influenced post–World War II Pentecostal faith healers. Among the Pentecostal faith healers influenced by Kenyon's writings were William M. Branham, T. L. Osborn, and Kenneth Hagin.[7] Hagin, the most noteworthy of Kenyon's disciples, gave voice to his teachings. According to McConnell, Hagin's writings, in many

---

[5]Kenneth Copeland, "The Force of Love," broadcast, TBN, February 5, 1986, audio tape #02–0028, 1987.
[6]Michael Horton, *Christless Christianity* (Grand Rapids, MI: Baker Books, 2008), 67–68.
[7]D. R. McConnell, *A Different Gospel* (Peabody, MA: Hendrickson, 1988).

instances, virtually quoted Kenyon's books verbatim. McConnell cites Christian Science, New Thought, Unity School of Christianity, and Science of the Mind as the major influences on Kenyon's theology.[8] Hagin dovetailed Kenyon's metaphysical cultic teaching into the faith healing branch of Pentecostal thought, thus becoming the granddaddy of that movement. Among those who pay homage to Hagin as their theological mentor are Kenneth Copeland, Benny Hinn, and Fred Price. The popularity of these three prosperity preachers took the teachings of Kenyon through Hagin to dizzying heights, inspiring many preachers in their wake and spawning the growth of Pentecostal and non-Pentecostal churches committed to word faith doctrine. The prosperity gospel flourished because the seeds had been planted. But it also had preachers like Copeland and Price preaching dramatically with open Bibles. Only through erroneous expositions and Scripture twisting could they make their claims with biblical support. They claimed man was not merely the *imago dei* (image of God) but that human beings are gods in themselves, able to speak words that create or alter circumstances. If one can conceive it and believe it, then one can receive it. Teaching the power of faith and human words represents one road that has led to the acceptance of the prosperity gospel.

The other road harks back to the liberal theology of Harry Emerson Fosdick. Fosdick was ordained as a Baptist minister in 1904 and was appointed Professor of Practical Theology at Union Theological Seminary in 1908, a post he held until 1948. From 1910 to 1924, Fosdick also served as regular guest minister of the First Presbyterian Church in New York City. His preaching, teaching, writing, and radio ministries railed against traditional and orthodox Christianity with its emphasis on evangelism and its uncritical use of the Bible. He emphasized insights drawn from psychology, evolution, and modern political and social movements, accenting the ethical rather than the doctrinal aspects of the Christian faith. Fosdick was a very effective communicator. His book *Being a Real*

---

[8]Ibid.

Person (1943) stressed the personal peace and power of religion.[9] Norman Vincent Peale, Fosdick's disciple, took things a step further with *A Guide to Confident Living* (1948) and *The Power of Positive Thinking* (1952). Peale's most prominent disciple, Robert Schuller, founded the Crystal Cathedral in Southern California. Although reared and ordained in the Reformed Church of America, Schuller unashamedly draws from the pragmatic pop psychology of Peale and Dale Carnegie in shaping his message, heard by millions through his enormously popular television ministry. Among his many best-selling books are *Self-Esteem: The New Reformation, Self Love,* and *Believe in the God Who Believes in You.* Joel Osteen seems to be the latest torchbearer of this man-centered distortion of Christian faith where God's will has been morphed into the American dream. Osteen is the pastor of Houston's Lakewood Church. With a winsome style, he preaches his brand of self-esteem and human potential to millions via his television ministry. Michael Horton has this to say about the message and meteoric rise of Osteen:

> Perhaps no greater example of the church's American captivity can be discerned than in the remarkable success of Joel Osteen. To the extent that it reflects any theology at all, his message represents a convergence of Pelagian self-help and Gnostic self-deification. If a bland moralism from Protestant liberalism became part of the evangelical diet through Schuller, Osteen has achieved the dubious success of making the "name-it-claim-it" philosophy of Kenneth Copeland and Benny Hinn mainstream. Osteen represents a variety of the moralistic, therapeutic deism that in less extreme versions seems to characterize much of popular religion in America today. Basically God is there for you and your happiness. He has some rules and principles for getting what you want out of life, and if you follow them, you can have what you want.[10]

In Osteen the two roads intersect—the one trod by Kenyon, Hagin, and Copeland on the one hand and the other one that flows

---

[9]Walter Elwell, ed., *Evangelical Dictionary of Theology* (Grand Rapids, MI: Baker Book House, 1984), 424.
[10]Horton, *Christless Christianity,* 68.

from Fosdick, Peale, and Schuller. Horton also offers another keen insight on the intersection of these seemingly divergent paths in the ministry of Osteen:

> There are no television healing lines, blessed prayer cloths or other eccentricities of yesterday's televangelism. Nevertheless, the key tenets of Word of Faith dominate his teaching, although it is communicated in the terms and ambiance that might be difficult to distinguish from most mega-churches and other seeker-driven ministries.[11]

I would like to examine the shifts within evangelicalism that have made prosperity theology less threatening and offensive. A good place to begin is the diminishing significance of doctrine among evangelicals. Perhaps a more accurate way of stating it would be the diminishing significance of the doctrines of historic Protestantism among an ever-growing number of evangelicals. As will be demonstrated below, this ever-growing number of evangelicals and prosperity theology proponents espouse doctrine that is decidedly different from the orthodox Christianity set forth in traditional creeds and confessions. In other words, doctrinal agreement between evangelicals and the prosperity gospel is often the result of evangelicals (and even word-faith teachers) departing from their doctrinal standards. This doctrinal departure is one of the steps on the road from liberalism. David Wells writes:

> In the United States this preoccupation with doctrine was one of the consequences of the bitter disputes with liberalism at the beginning of the 20th century. Liberals said Christianity was about deeds, not creeds. They said it was about life, not doctrine. Their conservative opponents, the fundamentalists, insisted that Christianity was about creeds as well as deeds. It was about doctrine as well as life. They came to define their distinction from liberalism, as they should have, in terms of their creeds and doctrines.[12]

---

[11]Ibid., 69.
[12]David F. Wells, *The Courage to Be Protestant* (Grand Rapids, MI: Wm. B. Eerdmans, 2008), 5.

Early twentieth-century liberals maintained that dogmatic defense of historic Christian doctrine stifled vibrant Christian living and created unnecessary division between them and other Bible-believing Christians who held to different doctrines on both primary and secondary issues.

In response, evangelicals held firm to certain core fundamentals, such as the inspiration and inerrancy of Scripture, the virgin birth of Christ, the atoning work of the cross, Jesus's bodily resurrection from the grave, and the second coming of Christ in final judgment. With these fundamentals at the center, evangelicals were able to reach beyond their denominations to cooperate with others in establishing colleges, conferences, publishing houses, and parachurch ministries. But as Wells observes, "What happened, though, was that this doctrinal vision began to contract. The goal that diversity in secondary matters would be welcomed quite soon passed over into an attitude that evangelicalism could in fact be reduced simply to its core principles of Scripture and Christ."[13] J. Gresham Machen, who was an early combatant against Christian liberalism, offered this cryptic if not prophetic warning: "The enemy has not really been changed into a friend merely because he has been received within the camp."[14] With the contracting of evangelicalism, many have been welcomed into the evangelical camp. "The unraveling of evangelical truth was signaled initially in an odd series of definitional tags that became evident in the 1980's and 1990's. That was when hybrids emerged: feminist evangelicals, ecumenical evangelicals, liberal evangelicals, liberals who were evangelicals, charismatic evangelicals, Catholic evangelicals, evangelicals who were Catholic, and so it went."[15]

Add to this list prosperity gospel evangelicals. The cover of *Time* magazine's September 17, 2001 issue featured a picture of T. D. Jakes with the question, "Is this man the next Billy Graham?" Whatever one thinks about the theology of Billy Graham, the point

---

[13]Ibid., 8.
[14]J Gresham Machen, *Christianity and Liberalism* (Grand Rapids: Wm. B. Eerdmans, 1997), 23.
[15]Wells, *The Courage to Be Protestant*, 9.

of reference is clear: just as Graham was the face of evangelicalism for at least two generations, Jakes may be the face of evangelicalism for the next two generations. The reason for such a lofty contemplation is the enormous popularity of Jakes and his successful television ministry, movie credits, best-selling books, entrepreneurial genius, crossover appeal, and community involvement. All of these are commendable, especially the latter. But what about his message? In the November 1996 *Charisma* magazine he spoke of people "who have failed to appreciate their divinity." He also implies that Jesus was a rich man, reasoning, "He had to be in order to have supported His disciples and their families during His ministry."[16] Both of these statements express the distorted (heretical) doctrine of word-faith teachers. Back when doctrine was more important to evangelicals, the fact that Jakes still holds to the modalistic position of his oneness Pentecostal background would have been enough to exclude him from the evangelical camp, but not in today's market.

Like the rest of the super-apostles of the prosperity gospel new breed, Jakes's sermons are emotionally charged pep talks that focus on human empowerment in overcoming life's obstacles while realizing one's destiny and potential. Two critical doctrines of historic Protestantism are undermined by such preaching: the doctrine of God and the doctrine of man. In commenting on the confusion of these two doctrines by the liberals of his day, Machen wrote, "God, therefore, it is said in effect, is not a person distinct from ourselves; on the contrary our life is part of His. Thus the Gospel story of the Incarnation, according to modern liberalism, is sometimes thought of as a symbol of the general truth that man at his best is one with God. . . . And modern liberalism, even when it is not consistently pantheistic, is at any rate pantheizing. It tends everywhere to break down the separation between God and the world, and the sharp distinction between God and man."[17] This failure to recognize "the sharp personal distinction between God and man" is at the heart of the prosperity gospel's emphasis on the power of human thoughts

---

[16]"Personal Freedom Outreach," http://www.pfo.org/jakes.html.
[17]Machen, *Christianity and Liberalism*, 63.

and words in changing one's destiny. "I believe one of the main ways that we grow in favor [with God] is by declaring it," Joel Osteen said in 2003. "It's not enough to just read [the Bible], it's not enough to just believe it. You've got to speak it out. Your words have creative power. And one of the primary ways we release our faith is through our words. And there is a divine connection between your declaring God's favor and your seeing God's favor manifest in your life. . . . You've got to give life to your faith by speaking it out."[18]

Here's an excerpt from one of Creflo Dollar's sermons in January 2005: "Words control the body. Oh glory to God! And regardless of what's going on in your physical body, you got to talk to it. I'm telling you I talk to my major organs. . . . I speak words to it. . . . The tongue in your mouth will control every inch of your physical body! Do not tolerate sickness and disease as long as you got a working tongue that can speak the established word of God!"[19] Both of these suave, immensely popular television preachers simply express the "old" doctrines of the prosperity gospel. What's clear is that these teachers ascribe to the words of sinful men a power that belongs only to God. But what may have been frowned upon by evangelicals in an earlier day has found a hearing in our day.

When orthodox doctrine is relaxed or even resented because it is perceived as being divisive (when it is actually serving a defining role), what remains is a religious atmosphere that unites around something other than the truth. One of the long-standing criticisms of old-school doctrinal preaching is its emphasis on sin and human depravity, which is perceived as negative and defeatist. So instead of human depravity and the need for a law-keeping, guilt-bearing mediator (Christ), prosperity preachers focus on human potential and the need to rise above adverse circumstances. It is precisely regarding the doctrine of God and of man that the Christian gospel and the prosperity gospel show their differences. If man's biggest problem is his sinful condition (which he can do nothing in his own

---

[18]Jackie Alnor, "Joel Osteen: The Prosperity Gospel's Coverboy," *The Christian Sentinel*, June 2003.
[19]See Forgotten Word Ministries blog at http://forgottenwordministries.wordpress.com/.

power to change), then his greatest need is a Savior who can do for him what he is unable to do for himself. The Christian gospel announces what God has done in and through Christ for man's salvation, which is given freely. The doctrines of substitutionary atonement, reconciliation, and the regenerating and illuminating work of the Holy Spirit are the constituent parts of the message. But the message itself is the announcement of what God has given and done in Christ for the salvation of His people. The prosperity gospel sees man's biggest problem as his temporal circumstances and physical condition; so its message centers on issuing commands to think positive thoughts, speak the right words, and follow the right steps in order to break through. Machen, contrasting Christianity and liberalism, says, "Here is found the most fundamental difference between Liberalism and Christianity—Liberalism is altogether in the imperative mood, while Christianity begins with a triumphant indicative; Liberalism appeals to man's will, while Christianity announces, first, the gracious act of God."[20]

The Bible teaches that God the Father and God the Son are the active ones, and people are brought to salvation by passively and humbly receiving by faith the gift of the Father in His Son (John 6:35–51; Ephesians 2:8–10). But Osteen says that we have to "grow in favor by declaring it. It's not enough to just read it, it's not enough to just believe it. You've got to speak it out."[21] Here's another Osteen imperative: "Keep a good attitude and do the right thing even when it's hard. When you do that you are passing the test. And God promises you your marked moments are on their way."[22] No matter how exciting the carrot at the end of the stick may be, imperatives are law and not gospel. Americans in particular seem to be prone to such imperatives because we have enormous confidence in our individual and collective ability to accomplish great things. As Billie Holiday sang, "The difficult I'll do right now, the impossible will take a little while." We are the "can do" nation with a

---

[20]Machen, "Christianity and Liberalism," 47.
[21]Alnor, "Joel Osteen: The Prosperity Gospel's Coverboy."
[22]Ibid.

track record of great accomplishments against great odds. But when it comes to the things of God, we are like all of mankind—impotent and bankrupt, guilty before our sovereign Lord, Creator, and Judge. What is needed in that situation is a Savior, and the prosperity gospel adherents can only offer a pep talk. It might be claimed that the imperatives of the prosperity gospel are not in relation to salvation but rather have to do with victorious Christian living once a person is saved. However, given the prosperity gospel's conception of man, I doubt that is the case. But if it were, it indicates another problem, what Michael Horton has called "assuming the gospel" or taking the gospel for granted. Horton describes it this way: "The idea is that the gospel is necessary for getting saved, but after we sign on, the rest of the Christian life is all the fine print."[23]

The issue of assuming the gospel may cause many otherwise conservative Bible-believing evangelicals to listen to what the prosperity preachers are saying. Perhaps they are simply disregarding the absurd and spurious, instead clinging to the positive. That might indeed be the call for some, because orthodox doctrinal preaching has long been accused of missing the mark when it comes to the "real issues" of life. This especially seems to be the case in evangelical circles where it is assumed that the gospel is solely evangelistic. If the gospel is only for the lost, then what about the saved? The prosperity preachers offer their "you can do it" imperatives as the solution. But the apostle Paul takes a decidedly different approach. In his letter to the Colossians, Paul tackles the system of victorious Christian living offered by certain teachers in Colossae. His exhortation (Colossians 1:1–14) is that the believers would be strengthened in the knowledge of what God has given in the gospel of Jesus Christ—there is not one single imperative. He goes on in verses 15–23 to expound the excellence of the person and work of Christ. In 2:6–7 he says, "Therefore, as you have received Christ Jesus the Lord, so walk in him, rooted and built up in him and established in the faith, just as you were taught, abounding in thanksgiving." Paul's only imperative is to walk in Christ, being rooted and built up

---

[23]Horton, *Christless Christianity*, 120.

in the knowledge of Christ (which is "the faith" alluded to in verse 7). The need to be rooted and built up in the knowledge of Christ is because as life becomes difficult there will always be some teachers who are prepared to take us "captive by philosophy and empty deceit, according to human tradition, according to the elemental spirits of the world, and not according to Christ" (2:8). The means for spiritual empowerment offered by these teachers consisted in abstaining from certain foods and drinks, observing festivals, worshiping angels, and experiencing visions (vv. 16–18). Paul says, "These have indeed an appearance of wisdom in promoting self-made religion and asceticism and severity to the body, but they are of no value in stopping the indulgence of the flesh" (v. 23).

It's not a stretch to see the similarity between the troubling doctrines of the teachers in Colossae and the empowerment formulas and principles offered by today's prosperity teachers. In 2:9–10 Paul says, "For in him [Christ] the whole fullness of deity dwells bodily, and you have been filled in him, who is the head of all rule and authority." In verses 11–23 Paul expounds on our union with Christ, and he makes the point that Christ's victory is our victory. In chapter 3 the apostle begins his practical exhortations, which consist in a series of imperatives. Two things should be noted about Paul's imperatives. First, they follow the gospel indicatives. Paul begins with the announcement of what we have been given in Christ, not with what we ought to do or ought not to do. Secondly, Paul's imperatives are backdropped with this reasoning: because of our union with Christ, we were buried with Him and raised with Him, and He has canceled "the record of debt that stood against us with its legal demands. . . . He disarmed the rulers and authorities and put them to open shame, by triumphing over them in him" (2:14–15). In other words, we do not begin with the gospel for our salvation and then move on to something else for spiritual growth and maturity.

In his interview with Joel Osteen, CBS's Bryan Pitts quoted from one of Osteen's books: "To become a better you, you must be positive towards yourself, develop better relationships, embrace the place where you are." Pitts goes on to say, "Not one mention of God in that. Not one mention of Jesus Christ in that," to which Osteen replied, "That's just my message. . . . I'm called to help people . . . how do we walk out the Christian life? How do we live it? And these are principles that can help you."[24] The problem, as previously stated, is that Osteen's "principles" make assumptions about human ability that simply do not correspond to the reality of our fallen nature. Furthermore these "principles" are not much different from what can be found in pop psychology and the motivational speaking circuit. It is what Michael Horton talks about in his chapter "How We Turn Good News into Good Advice."[25]

Prosperity theology's confusion on the doctrines of God and of man is seen not only in their imperative-laden gospel but also in the broad area of divine providence. Question 27 of the Heidelberg Catechism asks, "What do you understand by the providence of God?" The answer says, "The almighty and everywhere present power of God, whereby, as it were by His hand, He still upholds heaven and earth, with all creatures; and so governs them, that herbs and grass, rain and drought, fruitful and barren years, meat and drink, health and sickness, riches and poverty, yea, all things, come not by chance, but by His Fatherly hand." The follow-up question asks, "What advantages come from acknowledging God's creation and providence?" The answer: "That we may learn to be patient in adversity; thankful in prosperity; and for what is future, have good confidence in our faithful God and Father, that no creature shall separate us from His love; since all creatures are also in His hand, that without His will they cannot so much as move."

Fred Price espoused a different view: "God the Father cannot do anything in this earth realm without permission. Now again I realize that that statement is very as I say from an evangelical point of view (meaning the evangelical doctrines) . . . that this statement

---

[24]See CBS News website, http://www.cbsnews.com/stories/2007/10/11/60minutes/main3358652_page2.shtml?tag=contentMain;contentBody.
[25]Horton, *Christless Christianity*, chapter 4.

that I'm making that God can't do is like going out and committing adultery to them, it is sin."[26] One of the things about Fred Price and the prosperity teachers of his day was that they knowingly and unashamedly defied orthodox evangelical teaching. While the current group attempts to be less abrasive in their undermining of orthodox doctrine, the substance of their teaching is no less an assault on orthodoxy.

One of the things that stands out in the answer to the Heidelberg Catechism's question #27 is the acknowledgment that "health and sickness, riches and poverty, yea, all things, come not by chance, but by His [God's] Fatherly hand." This might be mistakenly perceived as fatalism by some. If a person stands in the rain for any period of time without proper covering, he will likely catch a cold. If a person habitually spends his paycheck on electronic gadgets instead of paying the rent, he is likely to be evicted. Theologians call this concurrence, which Louis Berkhof defines as

> the co operation of the divine power with all subordinate powers, according to the pre-established laws of their operation, causing them to act and to act precisely as they do. . . . It should be noted at the outset that this doctrine implies two things: 1. That the powers of nature do not work by themselves, that is, simply by their own inherent power, but that God is immediately operative in every act of the creature. This must be maintained in opposition to the deistic position. 2. That second causes are real, and not to be regarded simply as the operative power of God. It is only on condition that second causes are real, that we can properly speak of a concurrence or co-operation of the first cause with secondary causes. This should be stressed over against the pantheistic idea that God is the only agent working in this world.[27]

Berkhof summarizes the deistic position alluded to above by stating, "God's concern with the world is not universal, special and perpetual, but only as a general nature. At the time of creation He

---

[26]See http://www.letusreason.org/wf27.htm.
[27]Louis Berkhof, *Systematic Theology* (Grand Rapids, MI: Wm. B. Eerdmans, 1993), 169, italics his.

imparted to all His creatures certain inalienable properties, placed them under invariable laws and left them to work out their destiny by their own inherent powers."[28] It is clear from this that the prosperity preachers represent a deistic position on divine providence, which is due in part to the Pelagian legacy inherited from Charles Finney. The imperatives offered in the prosperity gospel are "invariable laws" that when exercised will bring about one's destiny. Fred Price says, "If you keep talking death, that is what you are going to have. If you keep talking sickness and disease, that is what you are going to have, because you are going to create the reality of them with your mouth. That is divine law."[29] In that case, it is the individual who determines the outcome either by speaking words that "create reality" or that "release" God's power. You can see how these quotes differ from Berkhof and the Heidelberg Catechism. But more importantly, these quotes differ from what is set forth in Scripture. In 2 Corinthians 12 Paul prays three times for a "thorn" to be removed from his flesh, but it was not (vv. 7–9). Instead Paul is told, "My grace is sufficient for you, for my power is made perfect in weakness," to which he responds, "I will boast all the more gladly of my weaknesses, so that the power of Christ may rest upon me" (v. 9). No amount of positive confessions or principles could alter what God clearly intended Paul to bear.

As noted above, there are laws of nature at work that God has ordained in the governing of human history. But Berkhof reminds us, "The laws of nature should not be represented as powers of nature absolutely controlling all phenomena."[30] It is God who is at work through these laws and not an inherent power in the laws. Christians should heed the biblical commandments in the ordering of their lives. While some adversity can be the result of wrong and sinful choices, some difficulties and tribulations simply cannot be explained. It is cruel, callous, and unbiblical to claim an understanding for all that a Christian may suffer in this life; it is appalling to

---

[28]Ibid., 167.
[29]See http://www.letusreason.org/wf25.htm.
[30]Berkhof, *Systematic Theology*, 169.

think that we have formulaic, man-made solutions to these very real hurts. The only viable help is to point the hurting soul to the gospel of Christ in Word and sacrament. It is there that God's covenant faithfulness is reaffirmed—sealed in the blood of His Son. The gospel reinforces the doctrine of providence, reminding believers that suffering does not mean lost favor with God or separation from His love. Consider the words of Paul: "But we have this treasure in jars of clay, to show that the surpassing power belongs to God and not to us. We are afflicted in every way, but not crushed; perplexed, but not driven to despair; persecuted, but not forsaken; struck down, but not destroyed; always carrying in the body the death of Jesus, so that the life of Jesus may also be manifested in our bodies" (2 Corinthians 4:7–10). Romans 8:28 clearly expresses divine providence: "We know that for those who love God all things work together for good." This leads the apostle Paul to explain the reason for such confidence in verses 31–34:

> What then shall we say to these things? If God is for us, who can be against us? He who did not spare his own Son but gave him up for us all, how will he not also with him graciously give us all things? Who shall bring any charge against God's elect? It is God who justifies. Who is to condemn? Christ Jesus is the one who died—more than that, who was raised—who is at the right hand of God, who indeed is interceding for us.

Having confidently explained that all things work together for good for the saints, Paul then teases out the implications of his confidence in verses 35–39:

> Who shall separate us from the love of Christ? Shall tribulation, or distress, or persecution, or famine, or nakedness, or danger, or sword? As it is written, "For your sake we are being killed all the day long; we are regarded as sheep to be slaughtered." No, in all these things we are more than conquerors through him who loved us. For I am sure that neither death nor life, nor angels nor rulers, nor things present nor things to come, nor powers, nor height nor

depth, nor anything else in all creation, will be able to separate us from the love of God in Christ Jesus our Lord.

This is why saints are exhorted to look with confidence outside of themselves to the person and work of Christ to be assured that their circumstances are governed by a loving, gracious, and faithful sovereign God. Question 1 of the Heidelberg Catechism asks, "What is your only comfort in life and in death?" The answer proclaims:

> That I belong—body and soul, in life and in death—not to myself but to my faithful Savior, Jesus Christ, who at the cost of His own blood has fully paid for all my sins and has completely freed me from the dominion of the devil; that he protects me so well that without the will of my Father in heaven not a hair can fall from my head; indeed, that everything must fit His purpose for my salvation. Therefore, by His Holy Spirit, He also assures me of eternal life, and makes me whole-heartedly willing and ready from now on to live for Him.

Prosperity theology teaches individuals to trust in one's own ability to change circumstances by applying prosperity principles, and this somehow activates God's power and favor. But biblical Christianity teaches that God's power and favor are at work, and His purposes are being accomplished even in the most trying circumstances. In considering the context of the prosperity gospel, let us be as clear and biblical in our analysis as Machen was in opposing the liberalism of his day. We are dealing with another gospel entirely. American evangelical beliefs have shifted so far that the aberrant gospel of prosperity theology has gained increasing acceptance within our ranks. Having forsaken the standards of historic Protestantism we have accommodated to the spirit of the age. Consequently today's Christianity retains some of the terms and forms of orthodoxy but with the substance of another gospel that is not the gospel at all.

So where do we go from here? Pastors are the first line of defense against the growing prosperity gospel movement. As a pastor I recognize the many struggles and pressures associated with the office. But I think it is necessary to don blinders to avoid characterizing our office by the example of "super-apostles." The title of one of John Piper's books captures the mentality we should strive for: *Brothers, We Are Not Professionals.* To this I would add, we are also not life coaches, cheerleaders, motivators, entertainers, or CEOs. We are under-shepherds overseeing the flock of the Good Shepherd. We are overseers of redeemed souls. We cannot afford to get distracted by the outward success of those who peddle another gospel and so lose sight of what the office we have been called to entails. We have not been called to be successful but rather to be faithful. My concern at this point is not with those who think that the prosperity gospel is authentic but with those who embrace the Christian gospel, yet believe that the prosperity gospel offers something.

Both the methods and the message of our office have been established for us. Paul encourages Timothy, "I charge you in the presence of God and of Christ Jesus, who is to judge the living and the dead, and by his appearing and his kingdom: preach the word; be ready in season and out of season; reprove, rebuke, and exhort, with complete patience and teaching. For the time is coming when people will not endure sound teaching, but having itching ears they will accumulate for themselves teachers to suit their own passions" (2 Timothy 4:1–3). I'm sure that most of us heard this text preached at our ordination, but the days that Paul said were coming have arrived. Our office as under-shepherds requires us to faithfully carry out the task of preaching Christ clearly and consistently. We are to preach and teach the Word of God with the strength and maturity of the flock in view (Ephesians 4:11–24). I think if we are to stem the present tide, it must begin with pastors committed to preaching Christ and Him crucified, who accept the doctrines of orthodoxy, and who are vanguards of the name of Christ, not their own reputations. Brothers, we are neither social reformers nor community organizers nor motivational speakers. Let us heed the word of the Lord to Ezekiel:

And he said to me, "Son of man, I send you to the people of Israel, to nations of rebels, who have rebelled against me. They and their fathers have transgressed against me to this very day. The descendants also are impudent and stubborn: I send you to them, and you shall say to them, 'Thus says the Lord GOD.' And whether they hear or refuse to hear (for they are a rebellious house) they will know that a prophet has been among them." (Ezekiel 2:3–5)

For Christians who are not in ministry, now is the time to do as Paul challenged the Corinthians: "Examine yourselves, to see whether you are in the faith" (2 Corinthians 13:5). Examine the claims of the Christian faith as set forth in Scripture and in the creeds, confessions, and catechisms of historic Christianity. Examine what the prosperity teachers profess. But know what you believe and why you believe it. Don't be fooled by your emotions or by what you see, because emotions can be misleading, and the same is true for what can be seen. Christianity is a religion of revealed truth. The question is not first whether or not it works, but whether or not it is true. And Christianity *is* true. Be strengthened and built up in that truth, knowing that God has set his promises in that truth, which centers in His Son. Paul says in Ephesians 4:14 that being strengthened in the truth of Scripture is what brings us to maturity, "so that we may no longer be children, tossed to and fro by the waves and carried about by every wind of doctrine, by human cunning, by craftiness in deceitful schemes." The best defense against the myriad of false doctrines that pollute the religious landscape (and will continue to pollute it until our Lord returns) is knowing truth, trusting it, savoring it, growing in it, and being thankful for it.

10

REV. MICHAEL ERIC DYSON: AN ANALYSIS

Craig Mitchell

I find myself in a rather strange position in writing this chapter, because this is not the sort of thing that I usually do. Most of what I write is related to ethics, epistemology, economics, and biblical studies. However, when Anthony Bradley asked if I would do this article, I readily agreed. He asked me to do this chapter because both Dyson and I are Baptists. I agreed to do this article because I admire and respect both Bill Cosby and Michael Eric Dyson. This is not to say that I agree with either of them about everything, but I think that both of these men have important things to say. So this chapter will begin with a synopsis of Dyson's history. It will then focus on what Dyson has to say about Bill Cosby and his concerns. Finally this article will share my analysis of Dyson's argument. It is my hope that I will do a fair and balanced job in this chapter.

MICHAEL ERIC DYSON

Michael Eric Dyson is an ordained Baptist minister who served as a pastor in Detroit for over ten years. His time in this position ended, in his own words, because

> I've been booted out of the pastorate of a black church for attempting to ordain women, and given that my extremely liberal views on homosexuality run counter to the received wisdom of black theological lights, I must confess that my version of the faith

might provoke as many cries of heresy as it may win converts. I've taken to the pulpits around the nation for a quarter century to proclaim my vision of the gospel, one whose keystones are social revolution, racial and economic equality, intergenerational understanding, and gender and sexual justice.[1]

He describes himself as an intellectual, as opposed to a scholar or academic.[2] He is also a cultural critic and the Avalon Foundation Professor in Humanities at the University of Pennsylvania. How did he arrive at this place of fame and/or notoriety? It is the purpose of this section to explore Dyson's history to help us understand how his background and experiences have shaped his views.

Michael Eric Dyson was born in the ghetto of Detroit, Michigan, on October 23, 1958. He went to college in Tennessee. He started at Knoxville College, a historically black college, at the age of twenty-one. He then went to Carson-Newman, a small white Southern Baptist school. He writes, "Carson-Newman was a true baptism in Southern Baptist Theology and worldviews, many of which were sometimes racist, even as members of the academic community encouraged their students to nurture their spiritual faculties. But my time in east Tennessee was crucial to my intellectual development, and taught me to navigate some perilous racial and cultural waters."[3] He graduated from Carson-Newman in 1985 and entered the PhD program at Princeton University. He graduated from Princeton in 1993. Soon afterward he was hired and received tenure at Brown University. Then he became a full professor at the University of North Carolina.

It should be noted, however, that Dyson's influences were not limited by his formal education. His path was not a straight one, nor was it an easy one. He was expelled from a highly esteemed private high school, Cranbrook, and finished his high school edu-

---

[1]Michael Eric Dyson, *The Michael Eric Dyson Reader* (New York: Basic Civitas Books, 2004), xix–xx.
[2]According to Dyson, "An academic toils in the vineyard of higher learning, usually as a teacher who may also focus on research. A scholar is an academic whose focus is research. And an intellectual in higher education is an academic or scholar who swims beyond her specialty and embraces the surging waves of knowledge as they wash against entrenched disciplines." Ibid.
[3]Ibid., 9.

cation at night school. He was married and divorced at eighteen because he impregnated a woman eight years his senior. During the time of his marriage he worked in a factory, where he was influenced in other ways.

> When I went to work in the factory as a teen father fending off welfare, and with the hope of saving money for college, I got provocative instruction from workers who drilled the point in my head: learning is for liberation, and knowledge must be turned to social benefit if we are to justify the faith placed in us by our forebears. In between loading brake drums, and welding and balancing them, I got a strong dose of Marxism, but a homegrown version attuned to the gritty particularities of black working life. That didn't mean there wasn't high theory; there was theory aplenty, though it was tailored to our needs and driven by our aspirations as a degraded and oppressed people—but a people who resolved to rise up from their suffering through self determining struggle. I was awed by these grassroots intellectuals who stood their ground and defended their lives with their brains and their words. There wasn't a hint of anti-intellectualism among them.[4]

From the time he was twelve years old, Dyson was also heavily influenced by his pastor, Frederick G. Sampson. He writes, "It was Sampson, more than any figure in my life, who convinced me of the service that intellectuals must render. Sampson believed that those who breathed the life of the mind must serve the people in whose womb they came to exist."[5] Sampson read widely and related his ideas to the people in his congregation and community. Dyson adds, "It is because of Sampson that I believe that intellectuals must serve the communities we live and work in. We've got to look beyond a comfortable career, a safe niche behind academe's protective walls, and a serene existence removed from cultural and political battles that shape the nation's fate. But we must be willing to shirk the

---

[4]Ibid., xxvi.
[5]Ibid.

contemptuous pose of distant observer."[6] In other words, for Dyson the life of the mind should also be a life of social involvement. The life of the mind should require that one attempt to change things for the good. The life of the mind does not allow one to remain aloof from the concerns of the day.

Still another influence on Dyson was his younger brother Everett, who was imprisoned because of murder. Dyson believes that his brother is innocent of these charges and has done all that he can to free him from prison. As of yet he has been unsuccessful. Nonetheless this is the kind of experience that causes one to think of things that he would not have otherwise. Undoubtedly Everett's imprisonment has done much to shape Dyson's thinking on the miserable plight of black men in America. He writes, "It's undeniable that black men as a whole are in deplorable shape. The most tragic symbol of that condition, I suppose, is the black prisoner. There are so many brothers locked away in the 'stone hotel,' literally hundreds of thousands of them, that it makes me sick to think of the talent they possess going to waste. I constantly get letters from such men, and their intelligence and determination is remarkable, even heartening."[7] He finishes his letter to his brother in prison by writing, "No matter how much education I've got, this Ph.D. is no guarantee that I won't be treated cruelly and unjustly, that I won't be seen as a threat because I refuse to point the finger at 'dem ghetto nigger' (a statement made by black and white alike) who aren't like me. I'm not trying to erase class differences, to pretend there's no difference in a black man with a Ph.D. and a black man who's a prisoner. I'm simply saying I can't be seduced into believing that because I've got this degree I'm better."[8]

Finally, it appears that Dyson was also influenced, to a lesser extent, by Jesse Jackson. Dyson explained that Jackson made it clear to him that he must be able to translate his ideas to the common man. "To paraphrase Ecclesiastes, there is a time and a place for

---

[6]Ibid., xxvii.
[7]Ibid., 20.
[8]Ibid., 31.

every academic language under the sun—for the jargons, obscurantisms, esoterica, dialects, glosses, and inside meanings that attend their path. But there is also the need to write and speak clearly about important matters for the masses of folk who will never make it to class."[9] To this he adds, "Work that can be widely understood or that is relevant to current affairs shouldn't be automatically suspect or seen as second rate. As Jackson understood, our failure to make our work accessible may be as much the fault of intellectuals as it is the problem of a 'dumbed down' society."[10]

Michael Eric Dyson is a complex human being like all of us. Many things went into making him the man that he is. Consequently, he has much to say to us that must be heard if we are to hear all sides. I would like to close this section by quoting again from his "letter to my Brother Everett."

> Even now I think of myself as a ghetto boy, though I don't live there anymore, and I refuse to romanticize its role in its inhabitants' lives. Not even survivor's guilt can make me that blind. But being from the ghetto certainly leaves its marks on one's identity. Don't get me wrong. I'm all for serious, redemptive criticism of black life at every level, including the inner city. There is a difference between criticism that really helps and castigation that only hurts.[11]

We are now prepared to examine what Dyson has said about Bill Cosby and his comments on the black community.

DYSON'S ANALYSIS OF COSBY

Dyson's responses to Cosby were published in his book *Is Bill Cosby Right? Or Has the Black Middle Class Lost Its Mind?* This book was published in 2005, a year after Cosby gave his famous address at Washington, DC's Constitution Hall. One can summarize Dyson's analysis of Cosby in a few ways. For the most part it might be viewed as *ad hominem* or "attack the man," but I really think

---

[9]Ibid., xxviii.
[10]Ibid.
[11]Ibid., 31.

that Dyson was attempting to show us another perspective of who Bill Cosby is and why his statements depart from that reality. The only way to assess all of Dyson's arguments is by way of an extended book review. In this section I do not plan to cover every chapter of Dyson's book, but enough so we can hear what Dyson is saying.

Preface

The book has five chapters, with a preface, introduction, and an afterword. The preface has the subtitle "The Afristocracy versus the Ghettocracy." The ideas expressed in the preface set the stage for the rest of the book; so the preface is not something that the reader can afford to overlook. If one does so, then he is at an extreme disadvantage because he will miss the context that Dyson is trying to give the reader. Dyson goes on to explain that

> Cosby's remarks are not the isolated ranting of a solo rhetorical gun slinger, but simply the most recent, and the most visible, shot taken at poor blacks in a more-than-century-old class war in black America. His views are widely held among a number of black constituencies—it is not unusual to hear some black poor and working class members themselves joining Cosby's ranks in barbershops and beauty salons across America. But Cosby's beliefs are most notably espoused by the *Afristocracy*: upper-middle-class blacks and the black elite who rain down fire and brimstone upon poor blacks for their deviance and pathology, and for their lack of couth and culture.[12]

Dyson explains that the Afristocracy come from all aspects of the black upper class.[13] They seem to agree that something is wrong with the black poor and that something should be done about them. Until Cosby gave his speech at Constitution Hall, these feelings were rarely aired in public.

---

[12]Michael Eric Dyson, *Is Bill Cosby Right? Or Has the Black Middle Class Lost Its Mind?* (New York: Basic Civitas Books, 2005), xiii.
[13]Ibid., xiv.

Dyson distinguishes the Afristocracy from the Ghettocracy, characterizing the latter as

> . . . the desperately unemployed and underemployed, those trapped in underground economies, and those working poor folk who slave in menial jobs at the edge of the economy. The Ghettocracy is composed of single mothers on welfare, single working mothers and fathers, poor fathers, married poor and working folk, the incarcerated, and a battalion of impoverished children. Ironically enough, the Ghettocracy extends into the ranks of athletes and entertainers—especially basketball and football players, but above all, hip-hop stars, whose values and habits are alleged to be negatively influenced by their poor origins.[14]

Dyson's book is not only a response to Cosby, but to all of the Afristocrats whom Cosby represents. Dyson asserts, "I will dissect Cosby's flawed logic, reveal the thin descriptive web he weaves to characterize the poor, and address the complex dimensions of the problems he bitterly broaches."[15] He finishes the preface by arguing, "If Cosby's implicit claim is that the black poor have lost their way, then I don't mind suggesting, with only half my tongue in cheek, that the black middle class, of which I am a member, has, in its views of the poor and its support of Cosby's sentiments, lost its mind."[16]

Introduction: An Afristocrat in Winter

The introduction to the book is subtitled "An Afristocrat in Winter." In this section of the book, Dyson explains that while he does not view Cosby as a race traitor, he still thinks that Cosby's ideas are elitist, grounded in generational warfare, and ill-informed.[17] At the same time he thinks that Cosby is right to emphasize personal behavior. Nonetheless, Dyson argues that Cosby is hardly the person who should lead the charge of the Afristocrats against the

---

[14]Ibid.
[15]Ibid., xv.
[16]Ibid.
[17]Ibid., 2.

Ghettocracy. This is because "Cosby has flatly refused over the years to deal with blackness and color in his comedy. Cosby was defensive, even defiant, in his views, as prickly a racial avoider as one might imagine for a man who traded so brilliantly on dimensions of black culture in his comedy."[18] These comments cannot be taken lightly. He addresses some of these criticisms later in the book.

Throughout the rest of the introduction Dyson points out that Cosby's remarks "betray seething class warfare in black America that has finally boiled over to the general public."[19] Dyson argues that by airing our dirty laundry in public, Cosby let white leaders off the hook. Thus Cosby overemphasized the importance of personal responsibility while not dealing with any of the structural aspects of society that keep black people poor and disadvantaged. "Cosby also slights the economic, social, political and other structural barriers that poor black parents are up against: welfare reforms, dwindling resources, export of jobs and ongoing racial stigma."[20] Dyson also notes, "The characteristics that Cosby cites are typical of all families that confront poverty the world over. They are not indigenous to the black poor; they are symptomatic of the predicament of poor people in general."[21] According to Dyson, "The poor folk Cosby has hit the hardest are most vulnerable to the decisions of the powerful groups of which he has demanded the least: public policy makers, the business and social elites, and political activists."[22] This introduction shows what Dyson will delve into at a greater level throughout the rest of his book.

Chapter One: Speaking of Race—Or Not

In this chapter Dyson explores the many ways in which Cosby has avoided the issue of race and how, as a result, he is an unworthy critic of the race. Dyson begins this chapter by explaining, "For most of his career Cosby has avoided race with religious zeal."[23] Dyson

---

[18]Ibid., 3.
[19]Ibid., 5.
[20]Ibid., 7.
[21]Ibid.
[22]Ibid., 10.
[23]Ibid., 15.

then tells the story of Cosby's rise to prominence. He explains that Cosby concluded around 1964 that "he would discard the use of color in his comedy since it was little more than a 'crutch.'"[24] He did so because he viewed racial humor as divisive. Cosby focused on the similarities between races rather than the differences between them. An essential part of Cosby's rise to fame came with his role on NBC's *I Spy*. On this show Cosby cultivated the idea of color blindness, that color was of no significance and that he should be viewed without regard to color. This was Cosby's approach to all of his television shows. Nowhere is this more true than in his 1984 sitcom *The Cosby Show*. The television critics applauded the fact that there were no racial jokes or problems of prejudice. At the same time some from the black community saw that Cosby did not deal with any social issues confronting black people.

Dyson quotes Cosby from an article in *Ebony* magazine: "Negroes like Martin Luther King and Dick Gregory; Negro groups like the Deacons and the Muslims—all are dedicated to the cause of civil rights, but they do their jobs in their own way. My way is to show white people that Negroes are human beings with the same aspirations and abilities that whites have."[25] In response, Dyson concludes that Cosby's desires can be understood to a certain extent, but in the end Cosby has a responsibility to his race that cannot be ignored.[26] He adds that Cosby's responsibility stems from the fact that he is so gifted and has the ability to do what others cannot. All of this makes Cosby's refusal to take action reprehensible.

It must be said, however, that not everyone can be a leader. Certain types of leadership demand certain types of personalities and gifting. Sometimes these gifts are natural, and sometimes they can be acquired. Dyson argues that Cosby's refusal to lead black people in the past disqualifies him for that leadership now. However, Cosby made important contributions by showing that black people are like everyone else, with the same abilities, hopes,

---

[24]Ibid., 17.
[25]Robert Shayon, "I Spy: Comedian Bill Cosby Is the First Negro Co-Star in TV Network Series," *Ebony*, September 1965, 65; Dyson, *The Michael Eric Dyson Reader*, xix–xx.
[26]Dyson, *The Michael Eric Dyson Reader*, 21.

and aspirations as white people. These contributions should not be denied. At the same time, had Cosby made comments on race his whole career, he would certainly have more authority to speak on these issues. Perhaps it is better late than never, but Dyson has more issues to discuss where Bill Cosby is concerned.

Chapter Two: Classrooms and Cell Blocks

In this chapter Dyson explains that while Cosby has a reputation for being educated, that reputation should be questioned. Dyson shows that Cosby received his degree at Temple University because of his "life experience." His EdD from the University of Massachusetts at Amherst was also controversial. Dyson quotes Reginald Damerell, who served on Cosby's dissertation committee, as concluding that degrees like Cosby's "do not attest to genuine academic achievement. They are empty credentials."[27] Dyson uses all of this to begin his attack on Cosby's ideas on the black dropout rate.

Dyson points out that while Cosby argued that the American dream is a myth in his dissertation, when *The Cosby Show* became popular, he argued that the American dream is real.[28] The Cosby who wrote the dissertation thus appears to be separate from the Cosby who excoriated black youths for their high dropout rate. Cosby cites a dropout rate of 50 percent for black youths when it is actually 17 percent.[29]

According to Dyson, Cosby is not only wrong about black youths with regard to dropout rates, he is also wrong about the way the black poor go about parenting. Contrary to Cosby, poor black parents do not spend their money on Air Jordans rather than Hooked on Phonics. Dyson points out that Cosby's attack on poor black parenting is just as fallacious as the rest of his charges. Citing a study by Cook and Ludwig, Dyson explains that "black students dropped out of school only slightly more than white students, largely due to low family incomes or absent fathers. Cook

---

[27]Ibid., 61.
[28]Ibid.
[29]Ibid., 71.

and Ludwig discovered that blacks and whites with similar family characteristics cut class, missed school and completed homework at nearly the same rate."[30]

Finally, Dyson sets the record straight on the issue of black youths and the criminal justice system. Dyson describes Cosby's comments as "incredibly naive, mean-spirited, or woefully uninformed."[31] Just as Cosby's views of the educational system have changed, so has his view of justice. Whereas the young Cosby viewed the justice system as two-tiered, one tier for the wealthy and another for the poor, the old Cosby stood by the side of Martha Stewart to support her on her insider trading case.[32] Dyson explains that there is racial disparity in criminal justice, especially in respect to black males. The situation is perilous for black youths, particularly those already trapped in the justice system. "More than six in ten juvenile offenders in residential placement are minority youth. Minority youth accounted for seven in ten juveniles held in custody for a violent offense."[33] But rather than condemnation, Dyson believes what these youths need is compassion. After visiting a youth detention facility with his wife, Dyson commented, "As I read Cosby's words, I thought about these young people often trapped by forces larger than their minds can explain." Dyson believes that much more can and should be done for our troubled black youths than mere condemnation.

Chapter 3: What's in a Name (Brand)?

Dyson's purpose in this chapter is to deal with the part of Cosby's speech where he deals with how poor blacks have been naming their children. Cosby is also concerned with body piercing and the way that poor blacks dress. Cosby reminds the audience that we are not Africans and the people he is describing do not know anything about Africa. Dyson argues that Cosby fails to understand poor black youths and their need to express themselves. Dyson also

---

[30]Ibid., 86.
[31]Ibid., 88.
[32]Ibid., 90.
[33]Ibid., 96.

emphasizes the idea that Cosby's attacks result from his "class consciousness." This class consciousness is no different from what the
black elite has always had. Cosby needs to reevaluate his position
and show more understanding than he is currently showing.

The desire for poor blacks to give their children unique and
African names is another way for these families to express and
celebrate their African roots. According to Dyson, "The African
naming tradition was often extravagant, similar to traditions in
the African cultures blacks left behind. Besides secret nicknames,
there were secondary names assigned to blacks to distinguish them
from others with the same names on large plantations."[34] Some
of these names "were African only in the sense that they reflected
flair and creativity, not because they had direct links to African
culture."[35] Dyson notes that it was not until the 1950s that distinc-
tively African names became common and prominent. But with the
arrival of the civil rights movement, the adoption of African names
returned to a significant degree. Cosby's rejection of this practice
can be traced to his color blindness and his embarrassment before
white people.[36]

Chapter Four: Family Values
This chapter is perhaps one of the most interesting because it con-
trasts Bill Cosby as "America's Father" with Bill Cosby the actual
father. A large part of Cosby's speech centered around family values
and how they are lacking with the black poor. Dyson writes, "Since
Cosby has taken to singling out poor families for special censure,
his own family problems suggest that not only poor families have
moral crises that warrant examination. At the very least, his travails
should nudge him considerably toward humility and compassion,
while they should cause the rest of us to find object lessons in the
contrast between his pronouncements and his practice."[37] Dyson
cites allegations of sexual assault by Cosby, a daughter who strug-

---

[34]Ibid., 126.
[35]Ibid., 129.
[36]Ibid., 134.
[37]Ibid., 144.

gled with drugs and alcohol, and finally the allegations of Cosby fathering an illegitimate child. Each of these is a cause for concern, and together they paint a picture that is difficult to square with the Cosby with whom we are acquainted. These are the charges that Dyson aims at Cosby.

At this point Dyson shows that Cosby's attack is only the latest sally in an ongoing class war between the black elite and the black poor. "The truth is that the black elite, and in some cases the black masses, have always taken the poor to task for their poor parenting."[38] Citing a study edited by W.E.B. Du Bois and Augustus Granville Dill, *Morals and Manners Among Negro Americans: A Social Study Made by Atlanta University, under the Patronage of the Trustees of the John F. Slater Fund*, Dyson argues, "The responses to the condition of parenting in the early 1900s may as well have been snatched from the mouths of contemporary observers, parents and critics on every side of the ideological spectrum."[39] In other words, the modern critique of lower-class black parents is not new. This class warfare is not something that will go away anytime soon, but it is not helpful for anyone.

Dyson ends the chapter by quoting an earlier Cosby, who he believes needs to be revived. This Cosby is "a critical, clear, compassionate analyst, perhaps even an informal ethnographer, of the lives of the poor."[40] We must do what we can to help the poor and realize that family problems can afflict the rich just as easily as the poor.

Chapter 5: Shadow Boxing with a Scapegoat?
(or, Do White People Matter?)
Cosby has argued that black people can no longer blame the white man for his situation. Dyson believes, however, that "Cosby's position is dangerous because it aggressively ignores white society's responsibility in creating the problems he wants the poor to fix on

[38]Ibid.
[39]Ibid., 168.
[40]Ibid., 180.

their own. His position is especially disingenuous because he has always, with two notable exceptions, gone soft on white society for its role in black suffering."[41] Dyson's concern is that Cosby is, in effect, letting white people off the hook. He argues, "Cosby has never been comfortable confronting white society over the legacy of white supremacy. His emphasis on color-blind comedy, and his retreat from social activism, were as much about avoiding the discomforts of race—including, oddly enough, the responsibility to represent as a fortunate black the interests of other blacks—as they were about overcoming racism."[42]

Much of the chapter involves a review of the ideas of a younger Cosby, who "spoke powerfully about how racist white leaders foment tension between the races."[43] Dyson also explains that this younger Cosby had great insight about the struggle of many blacks who fought for justice and dignity. This younger Cosby also understood the pain and bitterness that many black people felt because white people did not accept them.[44] Dyson concludes this section of the chapter by writing, "Cosby's intelligent and unsparing dissection of white supremacy, a rare public gesture by this color-blind figure, offers stirring testimony against his present refusal to hold white society responsible for its role in black suffering at all, or more than perfunctorily, in asides that serve as begrudging concessions and preludes to more attack."[45] At some point, that Cosby changed into the present Cosby who refuses to be concerned with systemic racism.

Dyson attributes the cause of Cosby's change to his being a part of the black elite, who serve as moral cops. "They policed poor black communities from the pulpit, the lectern, the convention floor, and the fraternity and sorority hall, damning the pathologies they believed were ruining the reputation of the race."[46] These black elites emphasize the importance of self-help

---

[41]Ibid., 182–183.
[42]Ibid., 183.
[43]Ibid., 191.
[44]Ibid., 193–194.
[45]Ibid., 195.
[46]Ibid., 197.

while refusing to acknowledge the complexities and difficulties involved in racial uplift. Once again Dyson argues that Cosby's arguments are only the latest in black-class warfare. In the end Dyson concludes that the black poor need compassion and understanding rather than condemnation. According to Dyson, we cannot let the white man off the hook because his actions still affect black society.

MY ANALYSIS OF DYSON ON COSBY

In 2007 Bill Cosby cowrote a book with Alvin F. Poussaint titled *Come On People.* It is quite possible that I missed it, but nowhere does Cosby respond to any of the charges that Dyson makes against him. And I am not aware of any other place in which he responds to Dyson. This does not mean that he has not, but I have not been able to find it. So what can we conclude from this? Perhaps there is more than a little truth in what Dyson has had to say. Dyson's research and his contrast of the old Cosby with the new Cosby is hard to ignore. Dyson's examination of Cosby's personal history undermines the message Cosby is currently advocating, and Dyson's critique of Cosby's arguments brings the validity of Cosby's position into question.

So why does Cosby's speech cause so many to respond with affirmation? Perhaps it is because even if Cosby is the wrong person to make this case, there is still some element of truth in what he is saying. Even if he is inaccurate about some of the facts, there are some things of which we need to be reminded. Even if this is no more than class warfare, that doesn't mean that it is completely wrong. Like Dyson, Cosby is a complex and imperfect human being who is capable of great successes and terrible failures. It has often been said, "The best of men are men at best."

At the end of the day it is important that we have both Bill Cosbys and Michael Eric Dysons if black people are to progress to where we can and should be. I, for one, am thankful for both of these men and their contributions to my thinking.

AN ANALYSIS OF DYSON FROM AN EVANGELICAL PERSPECTIVE

While there is much that I admire about Dyson, I also realize that no one would consider him to be a theological conservative. As an evangelical I have a number of criticisms about his ideas. In this section I will try to shed some light on these ideas from an evangelical viewpoint.

Dyson is an advocate of black liberation theology. This is a postmodern approach to theology that is both a hermeneutic and an ethic. Postmodernity assumes that there is no objective truth, morality, or meaning and that reality is subjective. Postmodernism also assumes that power is found in the group or community of which one is part. Black liberation theology is a socio-critical approach to meaning, truth, and morality. Like all socio-critical approaches, black liberation theology assumes that there are two groups, the oppressors and the oppressed. The oppressors cannot hope to understand truth, meaning, or morality. These oppressors are wealthy and apart from God. Just as Jesus preached the gospel to the poor (Matthew 11:5), the only ones who can understand truth, meaning, and morality are the oppressed (or the poor). As such, Dyson's approach is not new or novel. This in no way suggests that Dyson does not have original or brilliant insights, but I am suggesting that Dyson's method is a road that many have traveled on in the last thirty years.

Black liberation theology approaches the Bible with what Jean Francois Lyotard describes as a "hermeneutic of suspicion." In other words, black liberation theology, like all liberation theologies, has been described as a neo-Nietzschean will to power over the text.[47] The author of a text is considered dead, and as such he has no rights. It is the reader who places his values and meanings upon the text. This means that only poor blacks, the Ghettocracy, can have an understanding of the Bible. Only those who can see through the lens of poverty and oppression can understand the truth of the Bible, because the Bible was largely written by and to poor, oppressed peo-

---

[47]Anthony Thiselton, *The New Horizon in Hermeneutics* (Grand Rapids, MI: Zondervan, 1992).

ple. Those who have not been oppressed, the Afristocracy and white people, cannot possibly understand what the Bible means because, as Matthew 19:24 says, "it is easier for a camel to go through the eye of a needle than for a rich person to enter the kingdom of God." Needless to say, the hermeneutics of black liberation theology do not subscribe to biblical inerrancy, authority, or sufficiency.

The ethics of black liberation theology assumes that only the oppressed black community can understand morality. It also assumes that oppressors, including white people and the Afristocracy, have, at best, a confused view of justice and what is good and right. These other groups are outside the community to whom has been given knowledge of good and evil. This means that they are completely incapable of learning what is wrong or right. According to black liberation theology, good is what is good for the poor black community (the Ghettocracy), and bad is what is bad for the poor black community. Obviously this does not square with an evangelical view of ethics.

Black liberation theology, like all liberation theologies, is compatible with (and is usually based on) communism. Dyson is an advocate of communism. In Latin America, liberation theology went together with communism like eggs and ham. This is because communism or socialism appears to be concerned with the welfare of the poor. In reality, however, communism and socialism offer nothing but poverty. Roy Fish, professor emeritus at Southwestern Baptist Theological Seminary, has described liberation theology as "changing the nature of salvation from eternal to temporal, from spiritual to material and from individual to communal." According to American historian Richard Pipes, "There exists a widespread but false notion that socialism and communism are merely up-to-date secular versions of Christianity. As the nineteenth-century Russian philosopher Vladimir Soloviev has pointed out, the difference is that whereas Jesus urged his followers to give up their own possessions, the socialists and communists want to give away the possessions of others."[48] The notion of class struggle is central

---

[48]Richard Pipes, *Communism: A History* (New York : Modern Library, 2003), 4.

214   KEEP YOUR HEAD UP

to Marxist thought. All of this makes Dyson's black liberation theology very compatible with his Marxism. It has been said that consistency is the obsession of small minds, but no one (at least no sane person) would accuse Dyson of having a small mind. When one considers Dyson's black liberation theology tendencies alongside his Marxism, it should come as no surprise that he views Cosby's ideas through the lens of the oppressor and the oppressed. His dichotomy of the Afristocracy and the Ghettocracy is completely consistent with a liberation theology heavily influenced by Marxism. In this light, Dyson makes even more sense.

In the final analysis, it seems that while Dyson is very good at pointing out that the Afristocracy is attacking the Ghettocracy, he fails to realize that he, as a member of the Ghettocracy, is engaging in the same behavior. Just as it is wrong for the Afristocracy to attack the Ghettocracy, it is also wrong for the Ghettocracy to attack the Afristocracy. It seems that part of his attack on Cosby is based on this oversight. Perhaps what is needed is for both sides to listen carefully to what the other side is saying. Clearly both sides are expressing things that are worth saying and worth being heard. If we as black people are to move ahead, such dialogue is not a luxury—it is essential for our survival.

CONCLUSION

This book is not the final word on these issues. These essays represent the beginning of a much-needed conversation initiated by Bill Cosby and Dr. Alvin Poussaint about the role of the church in meeting the needs of black communities all over America. Cosby and Poussaint laid a big challenge, and we believe the black church in America is uniquely positioned to offer hope. The post–civil rights movement's social pathologies that plague many low-income, black inner-city neighbors all over America issue a call for prophetic action. Forty years after the civil rights movement the black church has lost its role as the moral center of black life in America. The black church served as the mediator for understanding the social and political implications for one's dignity as a black person made in the image and likeness of God (Genesis 1:26–28). This book is the beginning of recapturing that voice for the sake of bringing liberation to men and women in our communities in order for them to be free to experience what God created human beings to be and to do.

If you were to gather all of the contributors to this volume in one room, you would find that we would not agree with each other on the details of what to do, but we do share the chief conviction that the black church in America is not dead and has a vital and necessary role in addressing the issues in this book. Without the church, the black community is doomed. The black community would not have persevered through slavery, Reconstruction, Jim Crow, or the civil rights movement without leadership and moral formation offered through the church. To think of a future black existence in America without the church would simply be unprecedented. The diverse denominations and views represented in this volume come from various parts of the black church and represent the rich opportunities of future conversations. We need to start talking. We need to get black theologians, pastors, churchgoers, and non-churchgoers to dialogue about the issues in this book and to discuss whether or not the church has anything to offer. These conversations must lead to concrete steps for change because time is of the essence.

The good news is that the message of redemption offered in the Bible offers the hope that black America has depended on for centuries. God can change our people and our communities as He did with all sorts of struggling people and communities in the Bible. We may have difficult challenges, but there is hope. As the rapper Tupac lamented in his song "Keep Ya Head Up," there is much reason for despair:

> To all the ladies havin babies on they own
> I know it's kinda rough and you're feelin all alone
> Daddy's long gone and he left you by ya lonesome
> Thank the Lord for my kids, even if nobody else want em
>
> 'Cause I think we can make it, in fact, I'm sure
> And if you fall, stand tall and come back for more
> 'Cause ain't nuttin worse than when your son
> Wants to know why his daddy don't love him no mo'
>
> You can't complain, you was dealt this
> Hell of a hand without a man, feelin' helpless
> Because there's too many things for you to deal with
> Dying inside but outside you're looking fearless
>
> While tears is rollin' down your cheeks
> Ya steady hopin' things don't fall down this week
> 'Cause if it did, you couldn't take it, and don't blame me
> I was given this world I didn't make it
>
> And now my son's getten' older and older and cold
> From havin' the world on his shoulders
> While the rich kids is drivin' Benz
> I'm still tryin' to hold on to my survivin' friends

And it's crazy, it seems it'll never let up.
But please, you got to keep ya head up[1]

It is the prevailing view among the contributors of this book that even in the midst of pain, suffering, confusion, individual and social sin, and human brokenness we are not left hopeless. As we read in the motto of the African Methodist Episcopal Church, the hope that Tupac laments is found when we understand the intersections of "God Our Father, Christ Our Redeemer, the Holy Spirit Our Comforter, Humankind Our Family."[2] Although the circumstances of the black experience in America have changed, God's way of dealing with those changes has remained constant. The black church has known this since the beginning. What is needed today is a courageous resurgence of women and men to say, "No, the church will not be silent and sit on the sidelines while our communities and our families decline." We need to say yes to the church's speaking and yes to God's having His way so that people can be healed, delivered, and set free.

If you find yourself not agreeing with every point in these chapters we encourage you to question us, challenge us, and invite others to discuss what we are bringing to the table. We certainly do not claim to have all of the answers for every struggling community, but we invite questions and the use of this book as a catalyst for dialogue, direction, and change. This book represents an attempt at a way forward. We must start somewhere, and it is our hope that these essays will encourage you and your church community to keep your head up, because there are fantastic opportunities ahead to bring about the type of change that will last into eternity.

---

[1]Tupac Shakur, "2pac: Keep Ya Head up Lyrics," *Metro Lyrics*, http://metrolyrics.com/keep-ya-head-up-lyrics-2pac.html (accessed March 22, 2011).
[2]Dennis Dickerson, "'Our Motto,' African Methodist Episcopal Church, http://www.ame-church.com/about-us/motto.php (accessed March 22, 2011).

GENERAL INDEX

abortion, 63, 172
absent fathers, 22–23, 44–45, 70–72,
  110–11, 117–18, 140–42
abuse, 76, 78
Adams, Kenneth, 74
adultery, 49–50
African-American history, 99–103
African-American identity, 21–22, 31–40
American dream, 87, 120, 126–27, 206
Apostles' Creed, 165–66
atonement, 56, 187
Augustine, 40–42

Beatitudes, 127–31
Berkhof, Louis, 191–92
biblical manhood, 108–18
biblical preaching, 132–33
black liberation theology, 212–14
Bryant, John, 38

catechesis, 38–39
church doctrine, 38–39
church history, 174–75
church membership, 39
civil rights, 101, 121, 164
class warfare, 204, 208–14
community transformation, 59, 134–35,
  151–54, 158–59
Copeland, Kenneth, 179–80
Cosby, Bill, 21–24, 29–31, 49, 63–64,
  68–69, 86–87, 104, 122, 158–59,
  162, 169–70, 201–17
creation, 33–34, 108–9, 146, 150
cultural mandate, 34
cultural retrieval project, 31–32
cultural transformation, 125–35

dignity, 33–35, 68–71, 120
discipleship, 97, 116–17
discrimination, 22, 87–88, 121
divorce, 52–54
Dollar, Creflo, 177–78, 180, 186
Dyson, Michael Eric, 29–30, 90–91,
  197–214

election, 150–51
employment, 23, 87–88

Erickson, Millard, 47
eschatology, 37
evangelicalism, 124–35, 183–86

faithfulness, 111
Fall, 34–35, 104, 139
fatherhood, 111–14
female identity, 141–42
Fish, Roy, 213
forgiveness, 53, 147–48
Fosdick, Harry Emerson, 181–82
Frazier, E. Franklin, 101

gangsta rap, 81–98
Glaude, Eddie, 31
God
  covenants of, 49–50
  glory of, 113–14
  image of, 33–34, 37, 47, 64, 109,
    120, 146–47
  intimacy with, 79
  kingdom purposes of, 37, 150–55
  providence of, 190–93
  reverence for, 50–52
  see also Word of God
grace, 138, 147–48
grandmothers, 106–7, 140
Great Society Initiative, 43–46

Hagin, Kenneth, 180–81
Hammon, Jupiter, 163
Harrison, Nonna Verna, 146
healing, 137–38, 142–48
health care, 26–27
Heidelberg Catechism, 190–91, 194
hip-hop culture, 81–98, 102–3
Holy Spirit, 36, 56, 148, 152–53, 187
homelessness, 23
homosexuality, 71–72, 76
Hooks, Bell, 66–67, 71, 76, 139–40
hope, 36, 57, 168–69
Horton, Michael, 180, 182–83, 188
Hughes, Langston, 122
humility, 57
Hutchinson, Earl Ofari, 30
Hymowitz, Kay S., 45

Ice Cube, 80–85, 90
idols, 35
intimacy, 61–80

Jakes, T. D., 184–85
Jay-Z, 103–4
Jesus
    person and work of, 55–56, 109,
        126–29, 167–68, 188–89, 194
    transformative power of, 57, 79–80
    union with, 145–49, 189
Jim Crow laws, 100–101, 121
justice, 91, 94

Keener, Craig S., 53
Kenyon, E. W., 180–81

Lane, Tim, 142–46
Lewis, Robert, 110
liberalism, 183–87
life expectancy, 23
Lincoln, C. Eric, 94

Machen, J. Gresham, 184–85, 187
Male Investment Plan, 38
Mamiya, Lawrence, 94
marriage, 47–56, 64–67, 116
masculinity, 99–118
McCall, Nathan, 123
McConville, J. G., 49–50
McIver, Joel, 83
McMickle, Marvin, 91–92, 94
morality, 162
Morgan, Joan, 88, 93
motherhood, 72–74
Moynihan, Daniel Patrick, 43–44

new heavens and new earth, 130

Obama, Barack, 119, 123
orthodoxy, 157–75
Osteen, Joel, 182, 186–90

parenting, 24–25, 51–52, 55–56, 74–76,
    97–98, 116–18, 139–40, 206–7. *See
    also* absent fathers; fatherhood; moth-
    erhood
Peale, Norman Vincent, 182
Pentecostal churches, 180–81
Piper, John, 195
Pipes, Richard, 213
politics, 172
Poussaint, Alvin, 21–24, 49, 63–64,
    68–69, 86–87, 104, 158–59, 162
poverty, 44–45, 85–89, 212–13

prayer, 58, 94–95, 131–32
Price, Fred, 190–92
prophetic preaching, 91–95
prosperity gospel, 177–96

Quinn, Eithne, 83

racism, 23, 28, 41–45, 100, 205
reconciliation, 58, 78
redemption, 35–36, 46–47, 54, 78–79,
    105, 109, 137, 142–45, 150–51, 216
resurrection, 37

sanctification, 36–37
Scazzero, Peter, 116
Schuller, Robert, 182
Serwer, Adam, 28–29
sexuality, 61–80
Shaw, William, 83
Sherlock, Charles, 47
sin, 33–35, 67–68, 139, 142, 147,
    186–87
slavery, 43–44, 100–101
Smith, E. Dewey, 137–38
social action, 93–94, 118, 164–65
social conditions, 84–85
Soloviev, Vladimir, 213
spiritual maturity, 97, 189, 196
spiritual transformation, 146–49, 153–54
Steele, Claude, 28–29
stewardship, 114–15
suffering, 139, 143

theological anthropology, 32–41
thug life, 105–6
Trinity, 55
Tripp, Paul, 143–47
Tupac Shakur, 106, 216–17

unemployment, 23

victim mentality, 21–29
violence, 25, 27, 84, 90, 141

wealth, 159–60, 169–70
Wells, David, 183–84
West, Cornel, 137
white supremacy, 23–24, 209–11
Wilkinson, Bruce, 178–80
Wilson, William, 85–87
Word of God, 157, 162–65, 172–73
worship, 110–11, 115

SCRIPTURE INDEX

Genesis

1:26	33–34, 47
1:26–28	108, 146, 215
1:27	33, 47, 53
1:28	34
1:31	33
2	33
2:15–25	108
2:22	64
2:23	64
2:24	53, 64
2:24–25	47
2:25	67
3	34–35
3:6–7	67
3:8–9	77
3:9	104
3:10	105
3:10–13	72
3:15	35, 79, 109, 152
3:21	78
5:1	33
6	109
12	150
12:1–3	48
12:3	35
12:5	48
12:15–16	47
12:17	48
12:18	48
15:4	48
16	48
19:6	53
19:9	54
24:4	48
27	111
28:2	48
29–30	48
30:4	48
30:9	48
49	111

Exodus

20:18–21	109

Deuteronomy

5:2	49

5:16	49
5:18	49
5:21	50
24	53
24:1–5	50

2 Samuel

5:1	53

1 Chronicles

22:2–19	112

Psalms

2:8	150
8:5–6	33
102:18	118
139	105

Proverbs

1	118
1:7	50
2:16–17	51
3:5–6	51
5:3–14	51
5:15–19	51
5:18	51
5:20	51
6:20–21	52
7:7	51
10:1	52
13:1	52
15:20	52
19:14	51
19:26	52
20:20	52
22:6	51, 97
31:10–31	51

Isaiah

33:24	152
61	142
61:1–4	19, 138, 152
61:4	148

Ezekiel

2:3–5	196

Micah
6:8   80, 89

Matthew
3:17   109
5:3   127
5:13–16   129
6:9   55
6:19   130
6:33   151
7:1–5   93
11:4–5   152
11:5   212
12:28   152
17:5   109
18:21–35   53
19:3–9   52–54
19:24   213
22:37–40   36
25:31–46   92
28:18–20   107, 116
28:19   150

Mark
1:15   35
2:10   152
5:2   138
8:36   156, 161
12:29–31   115

Luke
4:16–19   142
4:18   92
9:6   152
10:18   152
16:1–8   114
22:31–32   112

John
1:18   109
3:5   105
6:35–51   187
13:38   112
14:12   114
21:15–19   112

Acts
1:8   150
3:1–7   159
16   111

Romans
1:16   99, 111
5:8   115
5:10–11   42, 57

5:17   109
8   145
8:22–25   47
8:28–39   193–94
8:29   105, 109
16:25   152

1 Corinthians
1:21–24   173
2:3–4   57
6:19   179
15:3   56

2 Corinthians
4:7–10   193
5:17–21   111
12:7–9   192
13:5   196

Ephesians
2:2   139
2:8–10   187
4:11–24   195
4:14   196
5:18   56
5:26   110
5:29   110

Philippians
1:12–30   111
1:20–21   111
2:5   56
3:13   116

Colossians
1   145
1:1–23   188
1:9–23   151–52
1:15   105, 109
1:18   37
1:19–20   111
1:20   105, 115
1:20–22   109
1:27   57
2:6–8   188–89
2:9–23   189
3   189
3:10   36

1 Timothy
2:8   110

2 Timothy
1:7–8   110
2:2   107, 117

3:16–17   173
4:1–3   195

Hebrews
1:3   109
10:23   174
12:1–2   174

James
5:13–16   154
5:16   58

1 Peter
5:4   116

1 John
3:2   37
4:8   55

Revelation
1–3   111
2:1   111

ALSO AVAILABLE FROM
ANTHONY BRADLEY

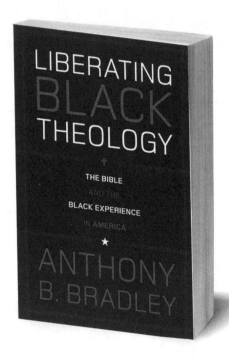